The Jim Santella Story
Father of Progressive Radio in Buffalo

By Jim Santella

Published by

BUFFALO
HERITAGE
UNLIMITED

Buffalo Heritage Press
266 Elmwood Avenue, #407
Buffalo, NY 14222
www.BuffaloHeritage.com
info@BuffaloHeritage.com
716-903-7155

ISBN: 978-1-942483-16-8 (softcover)
ISBN: 978-1-942483-17-5 (hardcover)
ISBN: 978-1-942483-18-2 (e-book)

Library of Congress control number available upon request

Printed in the U.S.A.

10 9 8 7 6 5 4 3 2 1

CONTENTS

This book is dedicated to Robert Santella.

My younger brother's heart was enormous and anyone who knew him was impressed with his smile, charm and good humor. Whether he was trying to get me drunk on my wedding day or lighting a cigar with a twenty dollar bill, he was impish and loved nothing better than to be devilish, even when the joke was on him. On his confirmation day he was decked out in a bright red robe that covered his pudgy preteen shape. When our uncle George commented that he looked like Friar Tuck, I couldn't help but add, "He looks like two fire trucks." No one laughed longer or harder than my generous sibling who grew into one of those effortlessly handsome men. He loved identifying me as his "younger twin brother," despite the fact that he was six years my junior. He took care of me as though he were an older brother, whether by giving me a hand during hard times or hiring me to spin records in one of the many Turgeon-brother restaurant clubs he managed. I know he is in heaven, probably scheming to give God a hot foot.

He was my brother, my hero, the wind beneath my wings.

ACKNOWLEDGEMENTS

This book would not have been possible without the help I received from many people.

My wonderful wife, Mary Lou, the love of my life, was absolutely invaluable throughout the entire writing and editing process. She was my tugboat, my motor, my anchor. ("Now will you stop twisting my arm, Mary Lou?")

My friend Karen Washbon worked with me on weekends for more than a year. She read chapters, made suggestions, and helped me organize the book. I could tell how well the writing was going by how many times I could make her laugh.

I'd like to thank my publisher, Marti Gorman, for her diligent work, cheery optimism, and steady "hand-on-the-tiller" guidance. If you like what you see, thanks go to art director Pauline Goulah. Assistant editor Jessica Gang receives credit for embracing the text. My long-time friend Dale Anderson gave the book its first read and offered valuable advice. Thanks also go to Mickey Osterreicher for providing valuable photos to choose from.

Thanks also to my loyal listeners who have supported me for so many years. Without you, there would be no book. Grazie mille!

Of course, I am responsible for any errors, misspellings, or meandering prose which make these acknowledgements necessary!

PREFACE

A smart, interesting friend on the radio. In that regard, Jim Santella is like many other great disc jockeys over the years. He's someone who has transcended the microphone and speaker to make the listener feel like they were having a real conversation. What continues to set Jim apart is his soft-spoken approach mixed with a strong, yet somehow universally appealing, sense of social awareness. As the voice and leader of Progressive radio in Buffalo for parts of three decades at stations like WYSL-FM, WPHD-FM, WGRQ-FM, WZIR-FM, and WUWU-FM, Santella led the rebellion against playlist conformity and management meddling. It more than once forced him up or down the dial, but people followed. Agree with him or not, like the music or not, a certain magnetism draws you into a Santella broadcast. It was a style that helped shape, and continues to shape, the sound of FM radio in Buffalo.

Buffalo Broadcasters Hall of Fame Induction Program, 2005

INTRODUCTION

I was born a child of radio, from classic shows like *Fibber McGee and Molly*, *The Jack Benny Program*, *Gene Autry's Melody Ranch*, *Dragnet*, *Suspense*, *Superman*, and *The Shadow*, to the modern-era music jocks of the 1950s on WEBR's *Sound of the City*, WKBW's George "Hound Dog" Lorenz, and WWOL's Guy King (a.k.a. Tom Clay), who played *Rock Around the Clock* for two hours straight, broadcasting from the ledge of the Palace Burlesque in downtown Buffalo in the summer of 1955. Radio, in all its variations, has been a constant companion, comfort, and addiction for me. Once I entered this magical world of music, entertainment, and information, it was the only life I knew or cared about. I was hooked.

Welcome to the wild but wonderful world of Buffalo's freeform radio, or at least the world of rock radio as I knew it. I was there at the very beginning: January 9, 1969, when progressive radio in Buffalo was born. Looking back on more than four decades of Buffalo's rock radio scene, I can't believe how quickly it has all passed. From rebellious hysteria to corporate seizure: *What a long strange trip it's been.*

It was a time when disc jockeys had the freedom to program a broad range of original music over the burgeoning FM band on stations that hadn't quite figured out what to do with FM frequencies. Unlike Top 40 AM radio, FM stations at that time stressed adult themes and variety, from blues-rock to avant-garde and the messages of the counterculture.

An actual set from my shift at WYSL-FM from February 4, 1971, included Traffic's "40,000 Headman," Fred Neil's "Mississippi Train," and Savoy Brown's "Sitting and Thinking." Jimi Hendrix's version of "Voodoo Child" followed The Fourth Way's version of "Voodoo Child." I threw in Maynard Ferguson's "Humbug," Bob Dylan's "Country Pie" from *Nashville Skyline*, and Lovin' Spoonful's "Nashville Cats." The set closed with "Waiting" by Santana, the Woodstock "Rainchant," and Strawberry Statement's "Give Peace a Chance." Nowadays "Stairway to Heaven" and "Free Bird" followed by ten commercials might pass for edgy programming. What happened? What killed the freeform music? It's easy to pinpoint the precise date that the "music died" for me, and it wasn't part of Don McLean's anthem, "American Pie."

Six days a week I would wake up thinking only about what music to play and what to say on my air shift. I'd arrive at the station an hour early to prep the show. Information was my stock in trade, regardless of the station or the format. My worn-out UB book bag was filled with the latest issues of *Rolling Stone, Creem,* or *Crawdaddy* magazines, counterculture favorites, as well as articles culled from various underground publications.

But in January 1975, uber consultant Lee Abrams' "SuperStars" format replaced music adventurists with a box full of prepared 3x5 cards and a playlist that stressed repetition over creative choices. It was "radio-lite." It was the beginning of the end.

FM radio had the potential to form a vocabulary of humanity. Playing music was my life! I've written about the factors and radio events that formed my encounter with the most engaging music to grow out of the 1960s.

And this, my friends, is my story.

I

EARLY DAYS

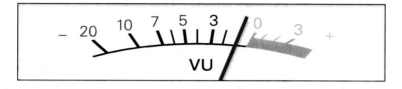

ONE

Child is Father to the Man

To borrow a line from the Rolling Stones' "Sympathy for the Devil," "Please allow me to introduce myself."

My name is Jim Santella.

But unlike Jagger's "man of wealth and fame," there was neither money nor notoriety in my family—although my father Dominic "Bucky" Santella was a Teamster Union steward back when labor had yet to find strength in unity. My mother, Mary (née Lobuzzetta), was what I like to call *immigrant strong*, meaning she could bench press me, my brother, my sister, and anyone foolish enough to take her on. Once when she was in her fifties, a young street punk flashed her on a city bus. She grabbed him by the short and curlies, bloodying his nose before the bus driver pulled her off of him.

My younger sister, Jerri, was equally feisty. Being the only female child in the family, she was sacrosanct. I still have bruises on my shins inflicted by her saddle shoes. Immunity was granted her because, in my mother's words: "You're the older one. You should know better." I still maintain she got a pass because she was a girl, not because she was younger. On the other hand, my "blood" brother, Bobby, suffered on three occasions from my fascination with throwing penknives into soft surfaces. The last episode happened one Sunday morning when Bobby made the mistake of taunting me while I was cutting slices off a loaf of Italian bread. I threw the bread knife at his pudgy calf. It punctured his thick corduroys and deflated my ego, as well. Fortunately for me, my father was still asleep and my mother was at church. Needless to say, I

Mary and Dominic Santella, circa 1935.

no longer carry a pocket knife.

Although both of my parents were born in America, they spoke Italian, but like many first generation European immigrants, they embraced the language and culture of their new country. Me, I was all-American, so much so that when Mrs. Calderella, my fourth grade civics teacher at P.S. 47 on Pratt Street, went around the room asking what nationality we were in an effort to make us more aware of our ethnicity, I piped up "African-American" because all my classmates were. When my mother explained that I was Italian-American, I was crestfallen. What would become of me? What was an Italian-American?

Later in my life, I'd discover that there were quite a few Italian-Americans who had made a name for themselves: Joe DiMaggio, Frank Capra, Frank Sinatra, Fiorello LaGuardia, and, later, Frank Sedita, Mario Cuomo, Francis Ford Coppola, Vince Lombardi, and JoAnn Falletta. I even learned about Caruso, listening to his music on Grandpa Santella's wind up Victrola.

I was born on April 24, 1938, too old to be a baby-boomer and too young to be a swing kid. It was radio that would save my mortal soul. I honestly can't remember a time without it. I adored our Motorola cathedral radio and all the magical sounds, shows, and stars that visited and entertained me through it. I discovered radio when I was two years old and movies when I was eight. They turned me into a dreamy child. I'd come home from school and listen to serials until supper. There were *This Is Your FBI*, *Suspense*, Orson Welles' *The Mercury Theatre on the Air*, and *Gunsmoke*. Jack Benny, Burns and Allen, and Bob

Hope sharpened my funny bone. From *Superman* to *Sky King, Jack Armstrong the All-American Boy*, to *Sgt. Preston of the Yukon*, I had the best invisible friends in the world.

Yes, it was radio that sparked the passion in me for show business, which was quite a contradiction, given that outside of our home I was painfully shy and had to attend speech classes as a child to cure a slight lisp. Yet, the gift of gab came easily to me. By the time I was eighteen months old, neighbors commented to my mom that it must be so nice to have company every day. In actuality, she had been carrying on full length conversations with me, or so the story goes. However, all I knew was that our living room console kept me company, entertained, and educated me. Between the worlds of radio and the silver screen, I grew up insulated in my ghetto neighborhood. But reality and puberty would change all that.

I was born on Buffalo's East Side, at 315 Sycamore at Spring Street to be exact. Growing up in the shadow of the Buffalo Forge Plant at Broadway and Spring, I was exposed to African-American music and culture from a very young age. Every Sunday the smell of barbecued ribs accompanied us on our walk to Grandma Santella's house for spaghetti and meatballs. We never owned a car, but the twelve block walk was worth the free samples that the neighborhood cooks offered to cute little me. While my mother slapped my back to make me walk straight, I was busy putting on my best waif walk. It always worked. Later, I realized it wasn't my performance that earned the tasty rib samples but simply the generosity of the neighborhood.

P.S. 47 was a mostly African-American grade school and on assembly days my classmates would bring in their forty-five rpm records. Most of them were R&B or blues records: Bobby "Blue" Bland, T-Bone Walker, Muddy Waters. We also happened to live across the street from a storefront Pentecostal Hall. The church ladies with huge hats decorated with feathers and ribbons were accompanied by sharply dressed men who wore pants with such razor sharp pleats that a wide-eyed kid like myself was bedazzled. When the exuberant gospel singing started, it was heavenly.

Little Jimmy in first grade.

Great music would come pouring out of that church. In a way, it was like having Aretha Franklin wake you up in the morning.

At the age of twelve, my comfortable world changed drastically. We moved to 103 Plymouth, in a predominantly Italian neighborhood on Buffalo's West Side. I had my own room, closet, and a dresser to store my baseball equipment, comic books, and the joke books I checked out from the downtown library. I couldn't read enough. It cost me a fortune in library late fees at a penny a book per day. It took me a while to make friends in the cliquish West Side neighborhood. To compound the problem, I rode the Sycamore bus back and forth from P.S. 47 to our new home so I could graduate from eighth grade with my classmates.

Stickball ended up becoming my introduction to the other kids in the neighborhood. I began to make friends on our street, and each afternoon I'd get home from school at around 4 p.m. and play stickball with them. My favorite two-person stickball game went something like this: one of us—the pitcher, would stand on the sidewalk across Plymouth between Jersey and Porter where the fire station was located. On the opposite sidewalk the batter would stand in front of the firehouse wall and try to hit the ball. Three strikes and you changed sides. My most vivid memory of this game found me switch hitting, a la Mickey Mantle, and poking one over the fence in front of the Methodist church. It soared past the trees and through one of the stained glass windows and we all ran away immediately. I don't know why we did the "right thing," but my friend Jerry Bellissimo and I decided to go to the minister and tell him what we'd done. It was my first lesson in "honesty being the right thing." We didn't have to pay for the damage, but we didn't play stickball against the firehouse wall for a long time either.

My friends and I liked to hang out on the street between Mr. Battaglia's grocery store on Plymouth and Jersey streets and Mr. Rizzo's grocery store on Plymouth and Pennsylvania. We called ourselves "The G's," short for "The Guys." It was Angelo Rizzo, the grocer's oldest son; Richie Gullo, the pharmacist's son; and Bobby Battaglia, whose father owned the other grocery; and me. Richie and Bobby wore the latest draped pants and wide lapel Mr. B shirts, named after jazz singer Billy Eckstine's sartorial splendor. Angelo and I looked like polecats in gunny sacks in our loose fitting, off the rack knockoffs.

Mr. Rizzo was our landlord and we lived in his two-family double, which permitted Angelo to sneak from his apartment into my apartment around 10 p.m. almost every night. We would listen to Angie's rhythm and blues records or WEBR's Bernie Sandler show late into the night. We were Bernie's most loyal fans, reveling in the honking saxophone of Big Jay McNeely and the R&B party music of the Trenniers. That was my introduction to the blues-based rock 'n' roll that would eventually dominate American popular music.

The gospel music I heard on Buffalo's East Side, combined with the jazz and R&B I heard on the West Side, helped to turn me into a life-long aficionado of blues-inspired music. It was those neighborhoods, as well as the city, that spawned jazz giants like Sam Noto, Don "Red" Menza, Louie Marino, Joel DiBartolo, Mel Lewis, Frankie Dunlop, Justin DiCiocio, Sam Falzone, Bobby Militello, and the list goes on and on. If you grew up on Buffalo's West Side in the 1950s, you heard lots of jazz and blues.

Another equally unique thing about my neighborhood is that world-renowned Kleinhans Music Hall, home of the Buffalo Philharmonic Orchestra, was right around the corner from our house. In fact, I could see the acoustically perfect structure from my backyard. As a teenager, my friends and I hung around the stage door and watched the musicians enter with their instruments. We couldn't see the performances, but we could hear them. The music would seep through the walls of Kleinhans and out onto Pennsylvania Street, Porter, and Normal Avenues. Yet, as a young teenager, this didn't seem extraordinary to me. It wasn't until I was an adult and started actually attending concerts that I realized how special those classical and popular musical memories were. I suppose you could say I was taking a music appreciation course painlessly. My neighbor, Mr. Bruno, even gave voice lessons to area students, adding to the musical atmosphere.

I was thirteen when I began attending Grover Cleveland High School. Grover had a student big band, led by Norm Weiss, our jazz-trained music teacher. The band was stocked with students from John Sedola's private jazz saxophone studio. If you took sax lessons from John, you

> Jazz great Red Menza was a senior when I was a freshman. He took lessons with Mr. Sedola for five years and was a monster sax player before he was old enough to vote. Upon graduation, he hit the road.

studied with the best. Almost all of his students were funneled through the school band, where they practiced daily from 10 a.m. to noon, five days a week, honing their chops playing hip Stan Kenton and Maynard

Ferguson big-band charts. I dreamed of playing the tenor sax and the drums in the band, but I was too self-conscious to take lessons.

At that time, we had a dress code, and there seemed to be competition among the boys to see who could dress the sharpest. Shirts and ties, spade shoes, drop loop pants—you name it, we wore it. Even poor little old me wore a tie, white shirt, and colorful pants. I remember saving money all summer from my two-dollar allowance to buy a custom-made suit from the local tailor, for the princely sum of $65. Yet, even the fancy clothes could not mask my shyness, and, sadly, the suit didn't make me any more popular. Walking down Niagara Street with my mother to shop for groceries on the weekend, I studiously avoided making eye contact with girls from my school that we passed along the way. I was as shy as a puppy, and I got teased about it by my street corner pals. Hanging out on the corner, my buddy Angelo would grab my nose and proclaim: "Hey, Slick, how come your nose is so cold—you in puppy love?"

It wasn't until I got a job as a busboy and waiter at MacDoel's, a popular downtown restaurant, that I was forced to overcome my self-consciousness. I cleared dishes from the counter, tables, and the Drum Bar Lounge, forcing me to come into contact with the customers. At first, I couldn't even look at them. But as the busy pace distracted me from my inhibitions, I started to relax. I came to realize that if I did my job effectively, I was invisible to the crowd. They couldn't care less about a teenaged, dirty-dish wrangler.

The longer I worked at the trendy restaurant, the more comfortable I felt. I even started taking drum lessons. It happened this way: the Main Street bus I took to work let me off in front of Wurlitzer's Music Store. Like a kid in a candy store, I'd look longingly at the Conn saxophones and the Gretsch drums. One day I didn't stop at the display window; instead, I walked right up to the counter and told the salesman, "I want to take lessons." I even surprised myself when I said it.

"What instrument?" he asked. I looked at the drums and then turned to the pearl grey tubs and sealed my fate.

"Drums!" Don Lillo was my teacher and in thirteen months I was good enough to play club dates and weddings.

Around this time, Steve Allen, the original *Tonight Show* host, replaced Bernie Sandler as my media hero. He was très hip, quick-witted, and played jazz piano. I used my drumsticks to accompany him on our telephone book. His guests included everyone from Sammy Davis Jr. to a young Frank Zappa playing a bicycle as a musical instrument—Zappa

I got so caught up in the beat lifestyle that I even attempted to grow a goatee, which I tried hiding with a Band-Aid. The night manager of MacDoel's, Mr. Sansone, was not amused. My fuzzy hirsute appendage was evicted from my chin. But it didn't disabuse me of my fascination with beards and hair.

was never less than avant-garde, no matter the circumstances, and little did I know that sixteen years later he would be one of my heroes.

The *Tonight Show* featured numerous rock 'n' roll artists in their earliest TV appearances. The show presented Elvis Presley, Fats Domino, Jerry Lee Lewis, Louis Jordan & The Tympany Five, and The Trenniers. I discovered the world of jazz and beatniks and took to it like a duck to water. I read about the beats in Jack Kerouac's *The Subterraneans*, William Burroughs' *The Naked Lunch*, and the lower case, postmodern poetry of e. e. cummings. I found inspiration in the unlikely relationship between Don Marquis' Archy and Mehitabel. Archy was a cockroach with the soul of a free-verse poet and Mehitabel was an alley cat with a purple past. Her philosophy for dealing with the vicissitudes of life was "*Toujours gai, Archy, toujours gai.*" Both of them demonstrated the free spirit of the beats.

After my shift at the restaurant, I started going to coffee houses like the Paralume on Pearl Street near Tupper. I listened to waif-thin female folk singers with long, straight hair sing politically charged songs like Pete Seeger's "Where Have All the Flowers Gone?," Woody Guthrie's "Union Maid," and The Weavers' "If I Had a Hammer.'

Watching television, I discovered there was a blacklist compiled by Senator Joseph McCarthy, who chaired the HUAC (House Un-American

Activities Committee), to deal with Communism and the rampant "red scare," that persecuted and ostracized writers like Dalton Trumbo and the Hollywood Ten. In the long run, the aggressive chairman of the committee, who conducted the witch hunt against liberals and homosexuals, was censured by the Senate on December 2, 1954, by a vote of sixty-seven to twenty-two, making him one of the few senators to ever be disciplined in this fashion. It was my first disenchantment with the American government.

Eventually, the shy James William Santella would morph from those beatnik roots into the longhaired hippy known as Jim Santella. The revolution took me from wanna-be jazz drummer to FM radio pioneer.

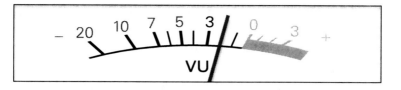

TWO

Radio Daze

No one ever taught me how to do radio, so I felt real comfortable with my lips kissing the microphone creating an intimate sound that wasn't planned but just happened.

– Jim Santella

I can't remember a time when I wasn't fascinated with all things radio. At thirteen, I built a crystal radio in the electric shop at P.S. 47. A crystal radio, also called a crystal set or cat's whisker receiver, is very simple; it needs no battery or power source and runs on the power received from radio waves pulled in by a long wire antenna. It gets its name from its most important component, a crystal detector, originally made with a piece of crystalline mineral such as galena.

At that time, grammar schools were run with the presumption that inner-city kids wouldn't be going to college, so we were provided with a woodworking shop, sheet metal shop, machine shop, and electric shop. Girls learned how to cook and sew in a fully operational third floor kitchen and sewing center. It was presumed that we would go on to McKinley Vocational High School, Burgard, Seneca, or one of the other manual arts schools.

Manual arts classes were not my strong suit—it took me a whole year to build the simple crystal radio, which consisted of copper wire wound around two six-by-ten pieces of wood, a headphone connector, a tuning device known as a cat's whisker, and hard plastic headphones. If it weren't for my bench partner, Carlton Evans, I might still be working on it. I knew nothing about it technically, but I was enchanted with the voices that came through the headphones, which looked like something a sailor in a submarine might wear. Reception was low, expectations high.

Years later I would delight in watching *WKRP in Cincinnati* and telling radio rookies who thought the TV show was unrealistic that it was created by Hugh Wilson who based it on his experiences working in advertising sales at WQXI-AM, an Atlanta Top 40 radio station.

Decades would pass, though, between building my crystal radio to watching radio on my TV. To be perfectly honest, I loved the magic that came out of the radio more than the mechanics of how it came out. Although the homemade crystal set was one of my prized possessions and proudest achievements, if truth be known, it picked up only five static-filled signals. Besides, for my sixteenth birthday, my mother and father gave me a deep chocolate-brown portable Zenith radio that seemed to pull in the world.

At sunset, radio stations that were licensed as "daytimers" were required to go off the air, reducing some of the electronic static that usually blocked the reception of distant stations. Radio sky waves bouncing off the clouds helped bring in distant voices all the way from Fort Wayne's WOWO-AM to Chicago's WCFL-AM: The Voice of Labor. Nowadays, with the Internet and iPhones shrinking the globe like a cheap pair of Walmart jeans, the magic of hearing radio DJs from hundreds or thousands of miles away is a blasé experience for the texting generation.

I went through batteries as fast as lightning on my Zenith—mostly trying to impress Carol Drago, the girl next door. Listening to Lucky Pierre on WBNY (located at that time at 1400 AM), we would talk for hours across the chain link fence that separated us. She was a senior, I was a junior, and we both took refuge in the rock 'n' roll music coming from my oxymoronic portable radio—the D-size batteries made it weigh more than my brother, Bobby, who hit puberty about this time with a thirty-pound weight gain.

Bobby teased me and Carol endlessly and eventually paid the price. On the day he made his Confirmation at Holy Angels Catholic Church, he wore an oversized red robe. My uncle George observed that he looked like Friar Tuck. I added, "He looks like two fire trucks," and the houseful of relatives gathered in the backyard roared. I got back at him. The incident became part of family lore and fueled my desire to be a comedian on Steve Allen's *Tonight Show*. It was at this time that I discovered my secret desire—I wanted to be smart and funny just like Steve Allen. I even took to wearing horned-rim, Buddy Holly-style glasses, just like Steve-a-rino.

By 1956, I was ready to graduate from Grover Cleveland High
School, attend college, and become
an accountant. Yes, an accountant.
You might ask, what about my funny/
smart dreams, my "secret desire."
Remember my immigrant-strong
mom? There was no way my mother's first child was going to waste
his life playing drums, telling jokes,
playing baseball, or anything else
that didn't lead directly to a college
diploma. I was expected to be the
first of the Santella/Lobuzzetta clan

In the attic of our Linwood Avenue home, circa 1956.

to graduate from college. Music was for kids. Adults got real jobs like a
doctor, lawyer, or accountant. However, the medical profession was not
for me—just the sight of blood made me queasy; lawyers weren't funny;
and Mickey Mantle showed no signs of leaving the Yankees.

Radio remained my not-so-secret joy, though. I knew it wouldn't turn
into, as my mother would say, a "real job." It was more like summer
vacation—you know, the lazy, hazy days of summer will always turn into
autumn, and you must return to the discipline of the classroom. No, radio
was not an occupation but an adolescent dream. Nevertheless, I was
hooked on the growing rock 'n' roll stations that were filling the AM band.

It was on July 3, 1955, when my first real rock 'n' roll radio memory
happened. I was barely seventeen when Tom Clay sprang his famous
billboard stunt on WWOL-AM:

Tom Clay, known on the air as Guy King ... climbs atop a downtown billboard seventy-five feet above Shelton Square. King,
microphone in hand, tells his teenage audience to drive downtown, honk their horns, and stop traffic while he keeps playing Bill
Haley and the Comets' "Rock Around the Clock." A huge traffic
jam ensues and Clay is arrested. He spends a night in jail but lives
forever in Buffalo's rock 'n' roll history.

(Anthony Violanti, *The Buffalo News*, March 24, 1996)

It was outrageous. It was spontaneous. It was out of control. I was hooked! I was a radio groupie long before the term was popular.

TEEN RADIO

Bernie Sandler was my connection to the wonderful world of watts, amps, and show biz. Bernie was a local disc jockey who had a popular music show on WEBR-AM. He played mostly jazz at night—which was when I loved to listen—but he also had a Saturday morning show geared towards teenagers. Calling him late at night, I would ask him endless radio questions—the anonymity made me fearless. I called him so often that eventually I managed to talk my way into an appearance on his Saturday morning show, which had a fifteen minute "Teen Report." I arrived an hour early and was surprised to find that he wouldn't be in until fifteen minutes before he was scheduled to do his show. I was led up to the second floor auxiliary studio where pictures of the station jocks lined the wall. I was awestruck. How do I get MY picture on that wall? I thought.

When Bernie came into his studio, he found me sitting in front of his RCA DX-77 microphone while the engineer was setting a level on my wispy, post-adolescent voice. He carried a thermos of coffee under one arm and a folder of commercials and public service announcements under the other. One of the PSAs had my name on it, but it was misspelled: "Jim Santora." Fortunately, the engineer had a correctly spelled copy, which he gave to Bernie. The microphone looked so cool that I

Growing up in Buffalo in the 1950s, I not only listened to Bernie but I even listened to Bob Welles' *Hi-Teen* on WEBR. I was only eight years old when the show went on the air in 1946. After moving to a few locations, including Kleinhans Music Hall, the show found a home at the Dellwood Ballroom at Main and Utica. That's where I attended the *American Bandstand*-style show, met a beautiful Hollywood actress by the name of Gloria DeHaven, and lost a milk-drinking contest. How could a growing young man concentrate on drinking milk when he was standing next to a goddess? She was the most glamorous woman I had ever seen. She smelled like my mom's backyard garden, only more mystifying.

hardly heard a word spoken to me, either on air or off. I read the PSA which plugged a hop at St. Leo's in Eggertsville, where three bands, The Premiers, The Ramblers, and The Dell Tones, were playing. On air, I introduced The Rhythm Rockers playing "Hurricane." On the way out, the program director, Dick Lawrence, shook my hand, said, "Good job!" and disappeared into the newsroom.

I would love to continue my radio odyssey by revealing that Dick hired me on the spot and I became the hero of my boyhood dreams, but that didn't happen. My fifteen minutes of radio glory seemed to be over as quickly as it began.

My radio dreams were put on hold for the next eleven years. If I could have turned my crystal radio into a crystal ball, I would have discovered that I'd become a college dropout after three semesters, I'd struggle through an unsuccessful marriage, and spend two years in Uncle Sam's army before returning to the University of Buffalo's School of Music. Instead, gentle reader, imagine a Hollywood film where a calendar shows the passage of time with months leaping off the page. Oh, by the way, this is where my radio feats should officially start with a clever chapter heading like: "Radio Feats Don't Fail Me Now."

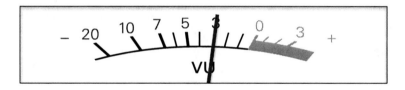

THREE

Feats Don't Fail Me Now

As you turn these pages, be advised that nearly seven years have passed from the fall of 1956 to September 1963. Let me hydroplane over this rough patch in my life: My plans to graduate from college hit a major snag. I flunked out of college after my sophomore year, got married in 1959, separated not long afterward, and was drafted into the US Army from November 1961 to August 1963, barely avoiding the Vietnam conflict.

Let's begin in 1956. My freshman year at the University of Buffalo was a landmark year for me. I immersed myself in poetry, political novels, and all things artsy. While working at MacDoel's, I met Carol Santucci, who called me a parvenu. I thought she was trying out her French on me. Come to find out, she was calling me an upstart or *arriviste*. Carol was an English major two years my senior. We shared a penchant for laughter and literature. She invited me to her renovated one-room basement apartment (on Mariner off of Allen Street), deep in the heart of the bohemia that was Allentown. Her friend Jack Christ, an abstract expressionist painter, occupied the apartment across the hall from her. The first time she invited me to her apartment, Jack was there sharing a bottle of Chianti. I was aware that they were lovers, so I was thrown off guard when she started to flirt with me. Jack was nonplussed and he added to my discomfort by teasing me with cautionary advice: "Be careful. She's going to seduce you."

Secretly, my unspoken response was: "Yes." And eventually she did. Carol was my first mature relationship and set the tone for my appreciation for intelligent women with a sharp sense of humor. I couldn't have asked for a more sensitive partner. I replaced Jack in her heart and hearth. I was drifting farther away from the family-oriented security of my West Side neighborhood. My pals and stickball were replaced by romantic poets, beat culture, and coffee houses. My foray into the world of politics was sharpened by my fascination with the HUAC trials in Washington, even though by now they were in decline.

I was only eighteen and still lived at home, even though I'd leave the house early and not return home until the wee hours of the morning. To avoid my mother's inquiries, I'd enter our house by the side door and sneak up to the attic where I would fall asleep in a spare room. It had a cot, my drums, and a Silvertone record player. By this time my parents owned a two-family home on Linwood near Delavan. I got used to sneaking into that room after a late night of partying. More than once I barely got settled in before my father woke up to go to work. When my mother asked me what time I had tip-toed in, I told her I didn't remember. She was wily enough not to press the issue. For better or worse, her first born was getting ready to fly the coop.

At this point in my life, the only radio I engaged in was listening to Joe Rico's midnight jazz program on WJJL-AM in Niagara Falls. Music and broadcasting seemed to be impossible dreams.

When Carol moved to New York City to pursue a writing career, I started dating her girlfriend, Jackie Keating. Like many young couples who marry in haste and think that they can repent at leisure, Jackie, my first wife, and I bought into the romantic philosophy that love conquers all. She was a painter. I was a musician. We went to coffee houses, listened to jazz, and read Camus. It was a match that love songs are written about—sad love songs.

Our relationship—an on-again, off-again affair—had always been shaky at best. When it took a turn for the worse, we solved our problems by getting married. Almost immediately we had money problems. I was trying, unsuccessfully, to balance the conservative demands of a married man and my desire to be a jazz musician. The ensuing years would be filled with false starts and mistakes, not to mention poor choices. What would I do without the requisite college skills to get a real job to support a family? All I knew was that I didn't want to wear a suit and tie and work in an office.

During my first year of marriage the only income I had was provided by my father's nepotism. Dad used his influence as a shop steward to get

Merchant Copy

THE BUFFALO
HISTORY MUSEUM

The Buffalo History Museum

1 Museum Court
Buffalo, NY, 14216

Bill To:

Shaun McLaughlan
, 14214

Cashier: James

Item #	Qty	Price	Ext Price
5671	1	$19.95	$19.95 T
Classic Rock, Classic			

	Subtotal:	$19.95
NYS Sales Tax	8.75 % Tax:	+ $1.75
	RECEIPT TOTAL:	**$21.70**

Credit Card: $21.70   XXXX4473
Mastercard   Expiry Date: XX/XX
Reference # 1000005009   Auth=71998B
Entry: Chip   Merchant # ***66941

Signature _____
    I agree to pay above amount according to card
    issuer agreement (merchant agreement
    if credit voucher).

AiD: A0000000041010

PLEASE RETAIN FOR YOUR RECORDS

Thank you for supporting TBHM mission to preserve
and make history accessible!

RETURN POLICY
All items are Non-Returnable.

14144

Merchant Copy

THE RECEIPT
HISTORY MUSEUM

The Buffalo History Museum

1 Museum Court
Buffalo, NY 14216

Bill To:
Shaun McLaughlan
13214
Cashier: James

Item #	Qty	Price	Ext Price
5871	1	$19.95	$19.95
Classic Rock Glass

Subtotal $19.95
(NY) Sales Tax   8.75 %   Tax   + $1.75
RECEIPT TOTAL $21.70

Credit Card: 5271 70...XXXX4470
Mastercard   XX-XX
Reference # 000035009   Auth=756498
Entry: Chip   Merchant # ***56041

Signature _____
I agree to pay above amount according to card
issuer agreement (merchant agreement
if credit voucher)

AID: A0000000041010

PLEASE RETAIN FOR YOUR RECORDS

Thank you for supporting TBHM mission to preserve
and make history accessible!

RETURN POLICY
All items are Non-Returnable

14144

me a union card and I worked out of the Teamsters Union, Local 375. As a dock walloper, I loaded and unloaded freight at the city's many transportation companies. I worked on call, averaging twelve hours a week at different sites. Jimmy Hoffa may have been getting rich but I wasn't.

Trucking companies were reluctant to pay benefits or overtime for a full-time crew. Instead, they would call the union office to supplement their full-time laborers. The method of hiring teamsters for jobs was called "the shape." It wasn't unusual to fill a shift with two or three full-timers and ten part-timers who collected no benefits. Taxes weren't withdrawn, meaning at the end of the year you owed back taxes. One year I filed thirty-six W-2 forms! We learned quickly how to "stretch the job." Picture "the shape" in the film *On the Waterfront*.

"Bucky" Santella at Associated Transport, Union Steward, Teamsters Local 375 in the 1950s.

One frigid, ten-degree-below-zero January morning, I was working alone in a refrigerated truck loaded to the roof with thousands of boxes of Birds Eye frozen food. No one order contained more than a dozen boxes. My job as a checker was to sort the orders onto four-wheelers and put them on any one of fifty-two loading docks. The work was tedious, demeaning, and colder than a witch's tongue. The next day, I turned in my union card. I was ready to go back to those warm college classrooms.

But Uncle Sam had other ideas. I was drafted in 1961. My uncles George, Jack, and Milt all gave me the same advice about the Army: "Shut up, make yourself invisible, and don't volunteer for anything." Sounded good to me. After all, they were survivors of World War II. I was sent to Fort Leonard Wood, Missouri, for eight weeks of basic training, followed by eight weeks of personnel school. They liked me so much, I spent eight more comfortable weeks in the Army's finance school at

Fort Benjamin Harrison, Indiana. I learned that the military runs on rules, regulations, and the chain of command. These skills kept me off the duty rosters, got me promoted, and allowed me to grow an unauthorized mustache. Maybe the Army wasn't so bad after all. WRONG! My permanent assignment to Fort Sill, Oklahoma, would be my undoing.

My first stop after reporting for duty with the clerk at C Company was to visit the next door barracks where the jazz riffs of a swing band bounced off the motor pool garage. The post band's duty was to practice daily. What an opportunity! I passed an open audition to play drums and waited for a transfer to my dream job. It never came. I couldn't get released from my desk job. I was deemed indispensable.

In my position as the battalion finance clerk, I was responsible for five hundred pay records. Soldiers really have only two concerns: their monthly pay and accrued leave time. I was responsible for both. Duty trumped drums. But on weekends, I'd regularly sign out a drum set from the entertainment center and gig off-post with musicians from the post band. I quickly developed a bad attitude and found myself on the short end of an early out due to my "failure to adjust." In the words of Pogo, "We have met the enemy and he is us." I was the recipient of an Honorable Discharge in August 1963. I traded in my Army helmet for a University of Buffalo (UB) beanie as a music major.

Returning home to Jackie, I found myself dropping her off at her parent's house. It was a do-over. I was unemployed, separated, and living with my parents. At least in the Army, I had some dignity, food, shelter, clothes, and a small paycheck that went far at the PX.

My parents fed me, gave me my old bedroom to sleep in, and didn't charge a penny. Lord, I felt like I was a teenager again trying to impress the girl next door! But my whole life was about to change, big time.

The year was 1963 and the fall semester was about to start at UB. I played jazz on the weekends and studied drums with John Rowland and George D'Anna, the two percussionists with the Buffalo Philharmonic Orchestra. I was at the music building from dawn to dusk.

While in music school, I got a full time job at UB's Lockwood Library. A year later, Jackie and I tried to kick the gong around once again. After living for a year in Fort Erie, Canada, as landed immigrants and maintaining our Buffalo jobs, we moved back to the States and put a down payment on a little Tudor home in Kenmore that we couldn't afford. I got dealt the "go to jail, go directly to jail" card. This time, we decided to forego another separation and jumped right to divorce. I learned my lesson. Love is one long, sweet dream and marriage is the alarm clock.

Actually, marriage was the best thing that ever happened to me. It produced my son, Joel, the pride and joy of my life. Named after my best friend, Joel DiBartolo, he was born in 1966. Like his namesake, my son, Joel, wasn't hesitant to talk truth to power. In later years, when I took him to a concert that I was emceeing, he patiently waited as I chatted with everyone from the musicians to the roadies to the audience. Finally, when his patience and good behavior were exhausted, he blurted out, "Dad, don't you ever stop talking?" What could I say? He was right. Another time when we were at an event where I spent more time chatting up several femme fatales than I did talking to my own son, he posed the question, "Don't you know any guys?"

After my divorce I moved in with Joel DiBartolo, who was a killer bass player who would eventually go on to play in the Marine White House Band, spend seventeen years in Doc Severenson's *Tonight Show* band, back up Carmen McCrae, and put in stints with the Buddy Rich and Maynard Ferguson big bands. His musical rap sheet would have made John Dillinger envious.

We shared a two-bedroom bungalow half a mile from UB; it was filled with jazz and blues albums that we played along with at all hours of the day and night. We learned how to play very softly; the neighbors were grateful. Three years of drumming with Joel in school ensembles as well as club dates, weddings, and jam sessions taught me more about jazz and music than any drum teacher could. I was fortunate to study with some of the best: John Bergamo, Jan Williams, Danny Hull, and Don Lillo, but Joel was my teacher, my mentor, and my close friend. He loved teasing me with an endless stream of drummer jokes that he'd tell me in the middle of a club date. I'd crack up, the leader would scowl at me, and Joel would pretend he was looking at the piano player's hands

> ## JOEL DIBARTOLO'S SENSE OF HUMOR:
>
> Q: What do you call someone who hangs out with musicians?
> A: A drummer. (Rim shot!)
>
> Q: What do you call a lady on a drummer's arm?
> A: A tattoo.
>
> Q: What do you call a drummer with half a brain?
> A: Gifted.

to figure out the chord changes. The real joke was that Joel had such big ears and played such perfect time that he made everyone play better. He had talent and shared it with all of us. We remained friends for life.

Joel was musically gifted. Me, I had luck. As much as I believe in the talent and genius of creative giants like DaVinci, Michelangelo, Beethoven, Einstein, and Woody Allen, there's no denying that for common folk like me, luck might trump the aforementioned brainiacs. I believe that luck has dogged my steps for most of my radio career. Let me give you a "for instance."

It was September 1965, one of those lovely autumn days in Buffalo when the leaves on the elm trees look as though they have been painted a verdant green, brown, and yellow. Even Rumpelstiltskin couldn't have spun such golden hues. I was leaving Baird Hall (now Allen Hall), which housed the Music Department and WBFO-FM, the student-run radio station at UB. I had just finished my marimba lesson with George D'Anna—the impish Philharmonic player was no teacher. His methodology was to play my lesson, blue eyes twinkling, then turn the mallets over to me with the admonition to "Loosen up, Ducky, relax!" George's thirty-minute lessons usually lasted twenty minutes, ending with my pocket-size percussion teacher giving me candy from his tweed suit coat.

That day he ran late, causing me to bump into Joel and his cousin Greg Perla coming from Norton Hall, the Student Union. Luck was about to trump talent. Greg was to be the stepping stone to my radio destiny. Joel introduced us; I recognized Greg's voice. He was the jazz programmer at WBFO and was about to graduate from UB. I was shamelessly aggressive, talking about Bird, Diz, Trane, Miles, Monk, Max, and every bopper I could think of. I wanted his job. I went so far as to tell Greg that if he ever needed someone to fill in on his jazz show, I'd be happy to. Remember, the full extent of my radio experience was my fifteen minutes of fame on Bernie Sandler's show.

A few days later, Greg called to offer me a shift playing jazz. I was ecstatic! He showed me the equipment and music library and told me to pick an hour's worth of jazz. The lesson lasted less than ten minutes: make a playlist, give the albums to the engineer, keep the jackets for liner-note information.

I showed up two hours early for my first shift. Greg never showed up. I was on my own, and that's the way it would be for the next forty-five years. To this day, I still remember the theme and introduction: Coltrane's

"Time Out for Jazz" at WBFO, UB's student station in Baird Hall's "two-story basement" studio in 1968.

"My Favorite Things" into, "Hi, I'm Jim Santella. It's five o'clock and *Time Out for Jazz*." Greg became a lawyer. I became a disc jockey.

WBFO's programing in the mid-1960s was eclectic to say the least. My jazz show was hammocked between a program on quantum physics and a show on Appalachian music, followed by local news. Remember, at that time there was no such thing as National Public Radio: no cable, no network programs. It was block programming, local in content, and locally produced. WBFO stressed variety and community coverage as originally envisioned by the 1934 FCC Communications Act, which suggested that radio be "in the public interest, convenience, and necessity." WBFO was student run and community oriented.

On weekends, Babe Barlow and citizens from the African-American community broadcast from a storefront studio on Jefferson Avenue. Babe was a WBFO blues host in the 1960s. Her real name was Lucille Brown, and at the age of five she was discovered in an orphanage by movie mogul Hal Roach. He cast her as Farina in his *Our Gang* movie comedies, and she appeared in other movies in the 1930s.

Programs, whether they originated from the campus or satellite studios like Babe's, were wide ranging, passionate, and reflected the social change that would usher in post-Kennedy America.

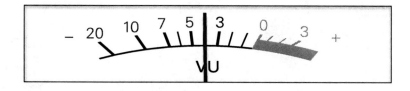

FOUR

Extension

WBFO usually went off the air at 11:30 p.m., but one day in 1967 at the weekly staff meeting, it was decided to extend the station hours and allow anyone who was willing to volunteer to do a freeform music show for as many hours as they could stay awake. As we started brainstorming a title for the overnight programming, I babbled something about extending the hours and *Extension* was born.

The format was simple: Show up. Play any kind of music for any length of time until the wee hours of the morning. If you felt like doing an hour show, fine. If you felt like doing four hours or longer, even better. Just run the sign-off and close down the transmitter when you were through. My personal record for longest shift was seven hours and fifteen minutes. I also held the station record for the shortest shift—thirty-seven seconds. I ran the :10 second recorded ID, started "Magic Bus" from the Who's *Live at Leeds* album, and before the vocal at :27, I ran the sign-off, shut-off the transmitter and put my head down on the broadcast board. A session with John Barleycorn earlier in the evening had sucker-punched me.

Shift length aside, it was a transcendental experience playing rock, jazz, folk, and classical music all in the same set. There were no limitations, no formats, no commercial considerations. I'd turn down the studio lights and do my shift in the dark. I mixed a milieu of music using a broad tonal palette. The challenge was to be musically egalitarian, not just weird.

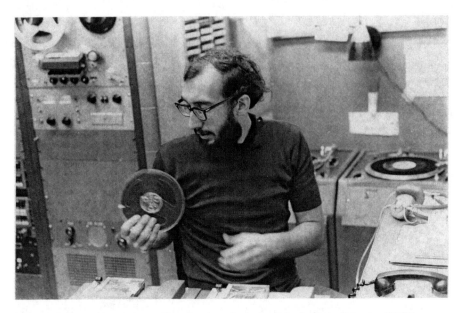

Reel-to-reel tape machines and turntables were the technologies of the day during Extension, WBFO's overnight freeform on-air experiment.

Igor Stravinsky's dark Russian rhythms found in his *Rite of Spring* would contrast and complement the existential lyrics and rock riffs of Cream's "Sunshine of Your Love." Miles Davis's "All Blues" and a raga by Ravi Shankar rounded out the rainbow of sound. Little did I know that I was learning a second language—the language of sound. At WBFO, I was free to explore music from around the globe. Nothing was too far out. I realized that we erect sonic barriers that exclude rather than include diversity. Being on the air three or four nights a week gave me the opportunity to experiment in my musical laboratory. Coupled with the burgeoning counterculture, Eastern philosophy, and rock 'n' roll music with a message, American campuses were becoming a center of political unrest. From Marshall McLuhan to Timothy Leary, Andy Warhol to the Maharishi, the world of communication was opening like a blooming onion.

That American popular music was maturing is evidenced simply by comparing the provocative lyrics of the Beatles' simplistic "Love Me Do" (1962) to Dylan's "Subterranean Homesick Blues" (1965):

Love Me Do – Lennon/McCartney

Love, Love me do
You know I love you

Subterranean Homesick Blues – Bob Dylan

Johnny's in the basement, mixing up the medicine
I'm on the pavement, thinking about the government

Both songs are exactly two minutes and fifteen seconds long. The Beatles use the word "love" twenty-four times; Dylan never uses it. Instead, he culls exotic couplets that range from No-Doze to coonskin hat. He also plays on the word "weatherman," as in: "You don't need a weatherman to tell which way the wind blows," to reference his "Blowing in the Wind" song, as well as both the meteorological definition and the violent wing of the antiwar movement. FM radio listeners were maturing from the Top 40 teenagers satisfied with the formulaic "bubble gum music" turned out by studio musicians, to more discerning music aficionados.

However, by August 5, 1966, with the release of their seventh album, *Revolver*, even the Beatles' love songs were transformed by their innovative use of the recording studio. Ten months later, in June 1967, *Sergeant Pepper's Lonely Hearts Club Band* revolutionized the way popular music was created. It was the atomic bomb of musical expression.

The Beatles had joined the musical, cultural, and political counterculture. Their one-dimensional love lyrics were replaced by sophisticated rhymes, innuendos, and a point of view. The Fab Four's densely layered studio recordings made it impossible to recreate their music live anymore. The medium had become the message. For my own part, I considered myself the messenger.

I have always credited WBFO for the start of my career. I was on the air five days a week for my hourly jazz show plus four nights a week for *Extension*. Even though this was volunteer college radio, it wasn't amateur radio. All the tricks of the trade and style elements that I honed during this period I would take and incorporate into my commercial radio career. It was this contribution and transition to the new radio style that would ultimately earn me recognition as an innovative, progressive radio pioneer and cement my place in Buffalo radio history. I always maintain, though, that I was neither the first nor the only progressive DJ in Buffalo.

II

ON THE AIR

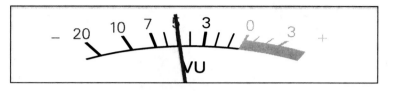

FIVE

WYSL-FM

In 1968, the McLendon Corporation's WYSL-FM adopted the new progressive rock format, hiring college students as disc jockeys. Buffalo's first underground radio station, WYSL-FM, would later morph into WPHD-FM. There was new music in the air, there was an audience for it somewhere, and McLendon wanted to be the one to get it. I would benefit from their decision.

Here's how I ended up on the air at WYSL-FM.

One day I walked into WBFO and there on the bulletin board was an ad: "Do you want to be a disc jockey?" I thought, Yeah, I'd love to be a professional disc jockey, who wouldn't? But this sounded like an advertisement for the "ABC School of Broadcasting" or something. I didn't really think they were looking for someone to work on the air. I had been led to believe that getting into radio was hard. My slow-paced delivery was the antithesis of Top 40 jocks. But I put together an air-check anyway with the help of Larry Osolkowski, WBFO station engineer, and it was just horrendous. Years later, I am still unable to listen to it.

I took British rocker Arthur Brown's "Fire" and inserted my name into his lyric: "I am the great god of hellfire and I bring you—Jim Santella!" I don't think I was full of myself, but I was full of something. Lo and behold, I got an audition.

It was August 1968. The Hotel Statler production studios were air-conditioned but I was sweating like mad. I was told by Paul Palo, the Top 40 jock in charge of hiring, to pick three songs to introduce. I chose three

My official broadcast license qualified me to take meter readings and clean the studios at WYSL-FM.

long cuts by The Band, Steve Winwood, and Cream. That's the music I had, that's the music I knew.

I started with the Cream album. I said everything I knew about Cream and "Sunshine of Your Love:" "Three lads from London: Eric Clapton, Ginger Baker, Jack Bruce … *Disraeli Gears* is the album … "Sunshine of Your Love" is the song." I'd always had music underneath me when I spoke on the air, a hold-over from *Time Out for Jazz*. It was pure luck and a surprise to me when I "hit the post" and talked it right up to the vocal. I thought I sounded like I knew what I was doing. Paul must have thought so, too. I knew he was impressed. Remember, there was no model for being an FM jock in those days.

Paul said: "I think I've heard enough. You've got the job." I was gonna be on the radio! Four months later a staff was hired. There were three full timers: Freddy Mancuso, George Hamberger (yes, that was his real name), and me. John Farrell and Cal Brady were our weekend part-timers. A library of long-playing albums was put together. My professional radio career began on January 9, 1969. Fast Freddy Mancuso started

In 1969, we broadcast out of the WYSL-AM production studio. The WYSL-FM station did not yet have a studio of its own.

things off at 7 p.m. He played four or five cuts from the new self-titled *Blood, Sweat and Tears* album. Years later I found out he was promoting the album for Columbia Records. At the time, I thought he sure knew how to pick hits!

My first show on WYSL-FM was memorable. I had the prime 10 p.m. to 2 a.m. shift. I thought I was calm, cool, and collected. I opened just like at the audition with "Sunshine of Your Love." "Three lads from London: Eric Clapton, Ginger Baker, Jack Bruce ..." with one important difference. My headphones weren't working. No problem. I continued anyway. I said to Paul, "Hey, these headphones aren't working!" He reached over my shoulder and flipped a switch. Turns out I never turned on my microphone. My first few minutes of my first commercial radio job would forever be aired as silence!

All of the artists whom we now consider rock's greatest stars were just starting out at this time. On WYSL-FM, we were playing albums— not singles like on AM radio—such as Yes, Frank Zappa, Iron Butterfly, Genesis, bands and performers who desperately needed a chance to be heard. Nobody played an eighteen-minute pop tune on AM radio. But progressive music could run as long as eighteen minutes, as evidenced by "Inna Gadda da Vida." Playing a song of such length was unheard of, but in 1969 the most requested song was that Iron Butterfly tune. It was so popular that sometimes I'd play it twice in a four-hour shift, as did the DJ before me and the guy who followed me. Did we overplay it? You bet your life. But people wanted it. The wild lyrics, hypnotic guitar riffs, and signature drum solo were just made for rocking out. Also, it was no secret that listeners used the music to enhance their drug experience.

There was no such thing as music you couldn't play. If we had it, we played it. We were just college kids who loved music. This privilege, to be at the right place at the right time and to be able to play whatever I wanted, made me think that it was my God-given right to play whatever I wanted. This notion would lead to no small amount of trouble later in my life.

A plus for my radio career was that I also happened to still be working full-time as a stack supervisor at UB's Lockwood Library, so I had a very good idea of what college students wanted to hear. It was an exciting and significant time on campus, and I don't think I have ever been as tapped into my audience as I was at that time.

It was then that I had my first opportunity to introduce a rock 'n' roll act on stage. The club was Uncle Sam's on Walden Avenue. Ultimate Spinach from Boston was coming to Buffalo. I got the album, memorized the names of the band members, and dressed up to go interview and introduce this band. Now picture this: I was wearing big bell-bottomed pants, a screaming green suit jacket, and short hair. I was so out of fashion that it was funny. The road manager was the first person I met and he introduced me to the band members. I can't tell you that I remember a lot about it, other than I kept getting the comment, "Nice suit." Hipper than hip was not yet my style.

Little did I know that my first professional radio job would last only a few months. It ended in May 1969 with me being fired. I went from hero to zero in barely four months. My goal was to make it to a year and be able to say: "Hey! I once worked in professional radio." I only missed it by eight months.

It happened like this: A weird friend of mine from UB came in for a visit while I was doing my shift. He said, "Introduce me to the overnight jock. Tell him I'm with the FCC." Now, why in the world would I do such an irresponsible, childish thing? Almost half a century later, I still blush at my stupidity.

As I went off the air, I cowardly asked the FM jock who followed me, George Hamberger, to explain to the AM DJ that my friend was not with the FCC. Well, somehow signals got crossed and that message never got delivered.

The next day, the overnight AM jock told the program director that we'd had a visit from the FCC. The McLendon Corporation called their attorneys in Washington. Their attorneys contacted the FCC. The FCC said they wouldn't send anyone out to a station like that, especially not at midnight. It didn't take me long to realize what had happened, and I had to quickly decide how I was going to handle it. I decided to tell the truth. I walked into the station manager's office and told him about the joke. He listened so sympathetically that I thought he was going to forgive me. Wrong! Instead, the message conveyed was more like "Don't call us, we'll call you. You will never work in this town again!"

Like George Washington, I could not tell a lie, but the truth did not set me free. Fortunately, I had WBFO to return to. And if it weren't for my poor judgment, I might not have ended up at Woodstock. So maybe being fired wasn't such a bad turn of events after all.

Sweet Baby James

Let me share two things with you. Thing one: what goes on in backstage dressing rooms stays in backstage dressing rooms. Thing two: things are not always what they seem to be.

It wasn't because we share the same first name that I've long been an ardent fan of James Taylor, although I do admit that being called "Sweet Baby James" by Melissa, a honey-haired eighteen-year-old Botticelli angel, did nothing to deflate my rickety ego. Truth be known, I discovered the future Mr. Carly Simon on his first Apple album in 1968 produced by Paul McCartney and Peter Asher. It was filled with allusions to mental institutions ("Knocking Round the Zoo"), drug references ("Steam Roller Blues"), and a longing for his North Carolina roots ("Carolina on My Mind"). I've always been drawn into his shy grin and autobiographical songs. No one, I repeat, no one can create stories that seem to be hammered out in the forge of spontaneity like James Taylor. Add a bluesy-jazz acoustic guitar accompaniment, vocals as affable as Kermit the Frog, and a delivery as buoyant as Miss Piggy, and the result is a journey that will take you through the art of songwriting from "Fire and Rain" and "Don't Let Me Be Lonely Tonight," to "Something in the Way She Moves" and "Sweet Baby James."

JT is the guru of masterful songwriting. His songs speak for themselves. But I want to tell you about the night I got waylaid backstage at the Niagara Falls Convention Center where Sweet Baby James was performing. Be forewarned that what follows is neither X-rated nor spicy. Saucy—yes, sexual—nope!

I arrived at the box office early to pick up my comps, only to be told by the cashier that there were no tickets in my name. That wasn't unusual. Promoters preferred to put VIPs on the guest list rather than give away actual revenue-generating tickets. Even comps are not free tickets—the band, the promoter, or the audience has to pay for them. I began to smell a rat. Just then, the promoter Eddie Tice appeared, winked at me, and teased me with "No tickee no seatee, Mr. Dee-Jay. But I know how you can get in the door." It turned out that his wife was as big a fan of James Taylor as I was. "If you would keep Kathy company, I would see my way clear to getting the two of you backstage passes to see James up close and personal." What a no-brainer. She was a charming beauty with a great sense of humor and an effervescent personality.

"Aren't you afraid she might run off with some good-looking radio guy?" I quipped.

"Yes, I am that's why I'm asking you."

"Touché," was my weak retort.

Eddie pulled two backstage passes from a wad as thick as the *New York Times* and Kathy and I were in. Behind the scenes, the sound man was tweaking the house system with endless repetitions of "Check, check, check." I blurted out "Cash, cash, cash," and Kathy smacked me upside my head so hard she knocked my cowboy hat to the ground. That's what kind of night it was. The roadies almost ran us over with a seven-foot guitar case that they were rolling downstage. I thought that if the guitar was as big as the case, Paul Bunyan would have a handful.

Fortunately, we decided to see James's entrance from the house, or we would have missed the spotlight as it came up on the guitar case. When the case swung open, out stepped Sweet Baby James with perhaps the most theatrical entrance of his career. "Steam Roller Blues" ignited the audience. The title of the song referred to a low-tech toilet-roll bong.

By the time the 110-minute set ended (encores included "Fire and Rain"), we were so drenched in perspiration that we would have made George Costanza seem hip. We dashed backstage to bask in the blue-denim-shirted singer and behave like two "tweeny-boppers." That's right. Not "teeny-boppers," but "tweeny-boppers." We vowed to get an autograph, but as the audience exited from the venue, our courage, resolve, and nerve drained just as rapidly.

"You go first, you're the dee-jay, the man with the words. I'll be right behind you."

"No way, I wouldn't be able to remember my own name."

"What are you, a man or a mouse?"

"Bring on the cheese!"

And so it went, the two of us at the edge of the stage as the roadies disassembled the lights, amps, and instruments. Paul, one of the security behemoths, arms across his chest, smiled at us like an indulgent parent and whispered, "You two are pathetic." He walked off toward the dressing rooms. He returned in less than a minute, pushed us toward a room with James Taylor lettered on the door and announced, "James wants to see you two." The die was cast. The fat was in the fire. Our goose was cooked. In short, we were ready to be exposed as the unabashed groupies that we were.

I entered the room and there he was: James Taylor. He walked toward me, put an autographed ticket in my shirt pocket and softly intoned, "Please, Mr. DJ, won't you play my song," a lyric from his hit "Money Machine." I was in hog heaven. I smiled back at him and nodded in the direction of guitarist Danny Kortchmar and bassist Lee Sklar. I felt comfortable and calm. I commented on the guitar case, his Apple debut album, and his ability to weave straw into golden lyrics. It was at that moment that I felt my ass being pinched. I continued chattering compulsively as I noted that none of the musicians in the room were close enough to reach me. Was it the security guard, a crew member, a roadie prankster, or just a weirdo? As I thanked James for the autograph and turned to leave, I noticed that Kathy was playfully beaming at me and it dawned on me that she was the culprit. We exited the room, I took two giant steps and demanded, "What were you doing pinching my ass in front of James Taylor?"

"I don't know," she said mischievously. "Maybe it was because you said how nervous you were and then chattered with James like you were fraternity brothers. I half expected to see a secret hand shake. So, I thought I'd give you something to squirm about!"

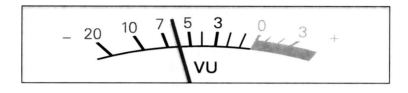

Going Down to Yasgur's Farm

It was the best of times; it was the worst of times. It was Woodstock, 500,000 screaming freaks, long-haired hippies, and music maniacs. For three days in August 1969, Max Yasgur's 600-acre dairy farm in Bethel, New York, became the birthplace of a nation forever embossed in the word "Woodstock." *Rolling Stone* listed it as one of the "Fifty Moments That Changed the History of Rock and Roll." Were you there? I was. It was a Kodak moment illuminated by lightning flashes. For me, Woodstock was a scrapbook of snapshots forever imprinted in my memory.

After only four months on the air at WYSL-FM, my dream job had come to a screeching halt when I pulled the rip cord on my broadcasting career with my FCC debacle. Since getting back into commercial radio seemed unlikely, I resumed my midnight shift at WBFO-FM five days a week, I also continued my full-time job at UB's Lockwood Library, and I enrolled in the UB Theatre Department full-time. You read that right: three full-time positions!

Here's how a typical day unfolded: As a stack supervisor at Lockwood on the UB South Campus, I was in charge of four full-time book stackers: George, Irv, David Parker, David Johnson, and a rotating crew of student assistants who seldom returned for a second semester of less-than-stimulating work. He may deny it, but *Buffalo News* arts editor Jeff Simon worked for me at one point. He usually could be found scrunched up in a corner, reading the books he was supposed to be shelving. Jeff was a compulsive reader, even then. The stackers, both student and full-time, returned books to five cramped floors of shelving. It was a tedious job that was easy to avoid by hiding in the nooks and crannies of the Greek-styled edifice. I was scheduled to work 8 a.m. to 4:30 p.m., Monday through Friday. I seldom arrived earlier than 8:15 a.m., checked to make sure everyone was working—they usually weren't. They knew my routine better than I did.

I wove fourteen credit hours of classes in and around my work schedule. I spent even less time attending classes than I did working in the library. Did I tell you that I took two liberal fifteen-minute breaks, one at 10 a.m. and another at 2 p.m., separated by a half-hour lunch spent at the student union? Some days my lengthy morning break encroached upon my lunch, and I ran so far behind schedule that I often went directly from lunch to my afternoon break. You might ask, what did you work on during those breaks? My radio show, of course. With so many information sources on the library shelves, it was like living inside Google. I was an info junkie, always on the prowl for material to incorporate into my show.

Truth be known, I was a terrible employee. I took advantage of the system. As a civil service employee, I knew that I couldn't be fired, short of blowing up the library or ignoring the "Quiet Please" sign. I carried more books with me to WBFO than most English majors carried to class. Yes, I got paid by UB, but I worked for WBFO. It took me many years to admit that indiscretion. Eventually, I learned a valuable lesson: You can't be a Robin Hood and be true to yourself. The worst lie is the one you tell yourself.

To remind myself of that truism, I had Shakespeare's quotation from Hamlet, "To thine own self be true," engraved on a silver ID bracelet that I wear to this day. I have to hold it up to the light to read the worn-thin words. It is the most important legacy that I will pass on to Joel, my son, and Marco, my grandson. It doesn't stop me from making mistakes; I just recognize them more quickly!

Fewer than thirty days after being fired from WYSL—on Friday, June 27, 1969, to be exact—I was back to my old tricks, broadcasting at midnight from the lawn in front of UB's music building and hosting a midnight picnic. I even supplied the free hot dogs, hamburgers, and soft drinks courtesy of the generosity of my brother, Bob, who managed a local Howard Johnson's.

As listeners of the late night WBFO radio program *Extension* already know, tonight is the night of the midnight picnic. Jim Santella, host of *Extension* to be broadcast live from outside Baird Hall, sees the event as an integral part of his bag.

And Jim Santella's bag is talking to people. And playing the kind of music he likes, and he hopes they like. He plays what he calls contemporary music. He doesn't like labels on music, and he plays all kinds with an emphasis on rock. And, of course, he talks.

Radio, the intimate medium, allows him to talk to people one-on-one. On his show he can and does rap about anything from getting parking tickets on campus to the role of the mayor of Toronto in banning rock music from that city.

(Mike Friedman, *The Spectrum*, June 27, 1969)

CALIFORNIA DREAMING

It was the '60s, which meant I was expected and encouraged to explore and experiment. I was either too idealistic or too naïve to realize that there were things I shouldn't do, so I went out and did them anyway. By this time, my hair was shoulder length, I had a peace sign buckle on my belt, and my shaggy beard reached down to my black Lou Reed t-shirt. Musically, I focused on the California underground rock that was bubbling to the surface of American popular music. I featured the Mothers of Invention, Jefferson Airplane, The Band, The Grateful Dead, Creedence Clearwater Revival, Jimi Hendrix, Janis Joplin—musicians who would dominate and revolutionize music trends during the '70s and beyond. Three music festivals proved to be the alpha and omega of the burgeoning youth culture: Monterey, Woodstock, and Altamont.

The Monterey International Pop Music Festival was a three-day event held June 16–18, 1967, in Monterey, California. The festival is notable for the first major American appearances of Jimi Hendrix, The Who, Santana, and the first large-scale public performance by Janis Joplin. The promoters saw the festival as a way to validate rock music as an art form. The organizers succeeded beyond their wildest dreams. Recognized as one of the beginnings of the "Summer of Love," Monterey also became the model for future music festivals, most notably Woodstock two years later.

ON THE ROAD TO WOODSTOCK

Here's how I got to go to Woodstock. Three radio buddies of mine from WBFO: John Farrell, Sir Walter Raleigh (a.k.a.: Walter Gajewski), Bernie Fromme, and I heard about a huge concert scheduled for downstate New York, August 15–18, 1969. The attraction was thirty-two bands, performing only 275 miles away from Buffalo. Wow! One thing led to another, and before we knew it, we were scheming for a way to get there.

Large-scale concerts had been going on since the Newport Jazz Festival in the 1950s, but Woodstock was destined to be the most influential one yet. The only problems we faced: no cash and no tickets. No problem. I called the number on the bottom of the ad which appeared in *Rolling Stone.* I reached the publicity people and asked for free tickets to "review" the event. I gave the call letters of the station, but purposely neglected to mention we were a college station. Three weeks later, four comps arrived, one for each of us.

On Friday, August 15, we wasted no time hitting the road in Bernie's less-than-reliable jalopy, a 1962 Ford Fairlane. We packed no clothes, no blankets, no tent, and no food. In hindsight, it was obvious none of us had ever been Boy Scouts. We were totally unprepared. I wrote the word "Woodstock" in my art history notebook and proudly propped it up in the rear window.

Bernie wore his favorite headgear, a striped stovepipe hat a la the *Cat in the Hat.* Bernie was a true zany with an unpredictable wit that knew no boundaries. He was an engineering student, complete with a slide rule hanging from his belt. He was our court jester, outgoing and affable.

John, on the other hand, was quiet with a rich, deep baritone voice that evoked Orson Welles. All he had to say was, "You're listening to WBFO" and he conjured up *War of the Worlds.* He hosted a classical music show but harbored a secret passion for rock. He was rail thin but blessed with a voice that rocked the heavens. God sounded adolescent in comparison. Eventually, I would be able to get him a weekend gig at WYSL-FM working overnights. Both of us favored candlelight to illuminate WYSL's cramped FM studio. The red light of the VU meters, combined with the orange-yellow candlelight, would have made Dracula feel right at home.

Sir Walter Raleigh, with his ever-present tobacco pipe hanging from his lips, somehow managed to look as neat and fresh by the fourth day of the festival as he did on the day we left Buffalo. He and I shared a common programming style, playing songs that made a political statement. For example, we might play "Revolution No. 9" by the Beatles and the Jefferson Airplane's "Volunteers," separated by Richard Nixon's *Checkers Speech*: "My fellow Americans, I come before you tonight as a candidate for the vice presidency. As a man whose honesty and integrity have been questioned ..." We would likely conclude the set with Country Joe McDonald's "Fish Cheer:" "Give me an F. Give me a U," etc. It was a perfect example of the whole being greater than the sum of its parts. Walter and I both kept extensive notebooks full of thematic songs, dialogue, and news clips.

ARRIVING AT THE SHOW: FRIDAY

Free admission was the best concert bargain, ever. Originally, tickets for the three-day event cost $18 in advance and $24 at the gate. Attempts to get people to pay were abandoned on day one when the fences were torn down. Woodstock was declared a free event.

We were among the last concertgoers to arrive at the festival grounds before the state troopers closed the roads around Woodstock. It was about 6 p.m. Imagine coming over the crest of a hill and seeing a vast ocean of hundreds of thousands of people. We had no idea how many there were, but it was, to put it simply, crowded.

We drove down a road and took a turn along some snow fencing. I think it was supposed to keep us out, but it didn't stop us. I remember coming across boxes and boxes of programs, given away free. I took two of the now classic programs. I still have them, in pristine condition. I wish I had kept my tickets too.

Time stopped. Or so it seemed to me. The next four days at Woodstock were spent listening to the music, getting soaked, and sharing the experience of a lifetime. Remember, cell phones, texting, and iPads were nonexistent. We got our news and information via stage announcements and from one another. It was supportive, it was insular, it was tribal. I even heard some people were getting high, indulging in some wacky weed. I don't know about that myself, but I got stoned on the music.

If you've ever been in the middle of a humongous crowd, you know how claustrophobic it can be. And after the first night of music, people moved in even closer—we eventually got within thirty yards of the stage.

My pride and joy Woodstock program. How in the world did it survive the Saturday deluge and the ensuing four and half decades?

Imagine sitting in an open cow pasture with hundreds of thousands of music fans, each separated by less than a yard. Although there was never a time when I felt threatened, I was always aware of the extreme intimacy; I've always been a little uncomfortable in a crowd.

When we first arrived on Friday, we had plenty of space for a couple blankets we found in Bernie's trunk that we all sat on. As the weekend progressed, our social space shrank until we were part of a sea of bodies that seemed to extend to the horizon. For the most part, the four of us stayed together. Bernie, Walter, and John proved to be more adventurous than me, though. One of us made a point of staying at our spot to keep our tiny kingdom from being swallowed up. Since I was particularly apprehensive of wandering too far from the comfort of our space, I usually volunteered to stay behind.

I don't think I roamed more than fifty yards in any direction, because I was worried about getting lost. Looking for a vacant Port-a-Potty was the extent of my adventurousness. Over the course of the weekend our kidneys were tested to the max. People looked so much alike to me; long-haired girls, guys with beards, cut off shorts, flowered dresses. It wasn't easy to get back to where you started.

John, Walter, and Bernie would be gone for twenty, thirty minutes at a time looking for food, drink, and adventure. Can you believe we brought nothing substantial with us? Just our jackets.

Realizing we left home with nothing to eat or drink, we had stopped on the way and bought two loaves of white bread, two pounds of bologna, a jar of peanut butter, and two large bottles of cola. Did we really think that was going to see us through the weekend? One meal on the road and one just before Richie Havens began his solo acoustic set pretty much wiped out our store of food. Obviously, we had little idea of what four hungry guys could consume. For the next two days I depended on Bernie's forays into the abyss to scare up food. I gave him $10 of the $50 I brought with me. That left me with $20 after subtracting my share of the gas money.

We were sitting almost dead center, only slightly off to the left of the stage, and pretty close in. Imagine sitting on the thirty yard line at Rich Stadium (now Ralph Wilson Stadium) at a Summerfest concert.

We decided to sleep where we sat so as not to lose our places. That is, except for John. On the first night he decided to walk way off into the darkness of the parking lots and sleep in the back seat of the car. There was no way I was going to go looking for our car in the middle of the night. John never told us how or even if he found the car, but for the next two nights he slept with us on the ground in front of the stage. He turned out to be the most resourceful of us, turning a plastic garbage bag into a raincoat to protect himself during the Saturday deluge.

With so many people, the dynamic around us was always changing. There was a lot of down time between acts. People would sit near us and chat for a while, and then, like flotsam on a sea of people, drift away to somewhere else. I always wondered, where did they go? To chat with another group? Head to their car and go home? Who knows? We discovered that the odds of running into people we knew were pretty remote. I never met any of the people I knew who said they were at Woodstock.

Hendrix, Joplin, The Who, Jefferson Airplane, Santana, The Band, and Crosby, Stills, Nash, and Young were high on my list of must-see performers. I thought most everyone else was frosting on the cake or I had seen them before. Thirty-two acts performed. I remember seeing twenty-three of them. For a long time I thought I had been awake from our arrival on Friday until we left on Monday morning. *Au contraire*. There were bands I don't recall seeing: Sweetwater, Bert Sommer, Tim Hardin, Arlo Guthrie, Quill, Keef Hartley, and Sha Na Na. None of them rang my bell as must-see performers, nor did they leave a lasting impression on the history of rock 'n' roll. I also missed Johnny and Edgar Winter, but I saw them often later in life, so I have no regrets there.

Did I have any disappointments at Woodstock? Only one. I was a huge Janis Joplin fan, but I slept through her entire set. Imagine that. I never considered Janis's singing soporific but I fell asleep waiting for her to go on. I caught just part of her last song, "Ball and Chain," and even that took on a dream-like quality. She died just fourteen months later, so I never did get to see her perform live.

I must admit there were a few surprises. Crosby, Stills, Nash, and Young's vocal harmonies were incredibly out of tune, I thought Melanie was out of place, and Jimi Hendrix was out of sight. He was a fitting conclusion to the weekend! But I'm getting ahead of myself.

The festival started more than an hour late. Richie Havens went on first. When Havens finished his set, he kept trying to leave but was told to do more encores. The next band was not ready. His song "Freedom" was improvised as part of this creative delay and became a worldwide hit.

The Woodstock Music and Art Fair was billed as "An Aquarian Exposition: Three Days of Peace and Music." The artists, craftsmen, and the counterculture were out in full force, from Wavy Gravy of the Hog Farm Commune to flower-power children who had migrated from the drug-soaked streets of San Francisco's Haight-Ashbury to sell their wares. It reminded me of the Allentown Art Festival.

Security was provided by the commune, which also provided hundreds of bushels of brown rice. They fed thousands of people at the Hog Farm Free Kitchen. I passed on tasting the brown, lumpy gruel.

There were a lot of stories about what was going on at Max Yasgur's farmland, which he explained in a brief speech on stage: "This is the largest group of people ever assembled in one place, and I think you people have proven something to the world. Half a million people can get together and have three days of fun and music, and have nothing but fun and music. God bless you all!"

However, not everyone made it to the birth of the new nation. Before the music even started late Friday afternoon, the thruways leading to the event were closed off by hundreds of New York's grey-uniformed state troopers. Who knows how many additional hundreds of thousands of fans might have shown up if uptight officials and monster traffic jams had not prevailed? By the end of the weekend, the neat Smokies and the mud-soaked hippies provided a stark illustration of the generation gap.

One of the performer "no shows" was Joni Mitchell. Later I learned she was invited to perform but turned down the offer when it conflicted with her scheduled appearance on the Dick Cavett TV show. She wrote the song "Woodstock" from what she heard about the event from her then boyfriend, Graham Nash. She stayed in a New York City hotel room watching national coverage on TV. Her imagination captured the moment with the truth of a prophet:

I came upon a child of God
He was walking along the road
And I asked him, "Where are you going?"
And this he told me...
I'm going on down to Yasgur's Farm,
I'm gonna join in a rock 'n' roll band.
I'm gonna camp out on the land.
I'm gonna try an' get my soul free.

We are stardust.
We are golden.
And we've got to get ourselves back to the garden.

(Excerpt from "Woodstock" by Joni Mitchell)

SATURDAY

The second day of Woodstock brought rain, nudity, and close encounters with feminine hips, breasts, thighs, and birthday suits. I didn't know where not to look. Let's just say, I would have felt out of place in the Garden of Eden.

As Quill started their set around noon, I was exposed to the generosity of the shared experience. A flower child who had brought snacks and talcum powder shared her modest cache with those of us surrounding her. She looked no older than seventeen. The teenaged earth mother, adorned in wide embroidered bell-bottom jeans and a camisole, was the picture of self-composure. I politely turned down her offer of the talcum powder, but she insisted it would protect me from sun stroke. How could I refuse her logic and kindness? She disappeared just as quickly as she had appeared, her huge leather saddle bag vanishing into the endless crowd. Ironically, the blazing sun eventually turned into rain.

Neither John, Bernie nor Walter was with me. They were out looking for the concession stands that were rumored to be running out of food quickly. When I told them of my encounter with the angel of mercy, they looked dubious. I think they thought I was hallucinating. The entire weekend had that dream-like quality. How else could one explain *The Peaceable Kingdom* behavior?

With storm clouds approaching, a chant went up, started, I believe, by Joan Baez: "No rain, no rain, no rain." It didn't work. After five inches of rain fell in about three hours, Woodstock became Mudstock. The slick

Years later I found out it was the flip of a coin that launched Santana's career. Michael Lang, one of the concert promoters, was given tapes of two bands auditioning for Woodstock. He couldn't choose, so he flipped a coin. It's a Beautiful Day lost.

There were many memorable moments at Woodstock for me. Joe Cocker delivered a soulful version of "With a Little Help from My Friends," digging deep into his Ray Charles influenced vocals—I really liked Joe Cocker and I've always thought it was a shame his career was so short. Another happened when The Who played late at night Saturday (or perhaps it was early Sunday morning), and Abbie Hoffman, radical leader of the Yippies (Youth International Party), provided one of the few overt political moments. He kidnapped the stage mic midway through The Who's set and harangued the massive crowd with, "Hey, this is all bullshit! John Sinclair of the MC5 is in jail for being caught with two joints!" He didn't get much further than that before Pete Townshend stopped him cold and Stratocaster-ed him off the stage.

You have to remember that this was before the days of arena rock, so compared to club-size concert spaces like the Fillmore East and West, The Hungry I, and The Wintergarden, Woodstock's stage seemed as massive as the great pyramid of Giza. Getting pushed off a platform that size could not have been pleasant. Townshend's actions basically said: You have a right to an opinion, now get off my stage! I don't ever recall seeing that exchange in the movie.

mud provided an exhilarating ride, or so it seemed. I chose not to participate. I was uncomfortable enough. Two of my most vivid memories are seeing hundreds of concertgoers sliding down the mud-soaked hills, looking like Neanderthals, and Santana's conga-driven set.

After the mud frolicking, a nearby pond served as a bathtub to wash off the adventurers. I was amazed at how comfortable everyone seemed drying themselves off naked, gathered around in clusters of grinning innocents. As for myself, I didn't even take off my rain-soaked T-shirt.

Bernie made the half-mile jaunt to where he had parked his car and retrieved a tarp he remembered he had stored in the trunk. By the time he got back, forty-five minutes after the end of the three-hour rainfall, Walter and I were soaked. John had found refuge with a group of concertgoers from Akron, Ohio, who had the foresight to pack a US Army surplus tent. The small refuge squeezed nine bodies in a space designed for two. It was intimate with four couples and John.

To the pessimistic outsider, bad weather, food shortages, and poor sanitation were the legacy of Woodstock. However, to those of us who were there, Saturday's highlights were the mud-sliding, the skinny-dipping, and Santana's electrifying set featuring the barely twenty-year-old drummer Michael Shrieve's solo during an extended version of "Soul Sacrifice." It is permanently stored in my memory banks.

THE JUNK YARD

My final image of Woodstock was of Jimi Hendrix dressed in an immaculate white fringed outfit which stood in sharp contrast to the mountains of dirt and debris surrounding him. The crowd had shrunk substantially by Monday morning, but those of us who stayed until the bitter end were treated to two hours of what would turn out to be vintage Hendrix as he spun out a solo of "The Star Spangled Banner" that could have been the clarion call of the weekend.

Piles of abandoned clothes, shoes, and junk littered the muddy farm land. What started out as a Garden of Eden had been transformed into a junkyard. Some of us clung to the last pieces of the dream, some stumbled around mud puddles searching for companions, and a few scavengers raked through the abandoned artifacts of a weekend that would turn out to be as mythic as a Greek tragedy.

Joan Baez, the Barefoot Madonna

Opinions are like belly buttons: everyone has one. So don't let your bull dog opinions run off with your puppy dog facts. We all believe that our opinions are sacrosanct. Even yours truly is not immune from substituting opinion for objectivity. This close encounter might seem to be about my admiration for Joan Baez, but it is really about making honest value judgments. What I like about the interview is that it quickly moved from the usual questions about touring to comments about her heartfelt dedication to social issues. Because I spoke to her in an open, honest manner instead of talking in superlatives, she responded in kind.

In 1975, I interviewed Joan Baez when she supported Bob Dylan on his historic Rolling Thunder Revue tour, which also included Joni Mitchell and Roger McGuinn. Baez won my heart, respect, and admiration with her classy intelligence and self-confidence.

In our hyperbolic world of "Entertainment Tonight," movie, music, and TV criticism often ride on a slippery slope of personal preferences or monetary goals. Just because your favorite supermarket tabloid says: "These are the top ten …" doesn't mean that list is objective. So, you need to be wary any time you see a "Best of" or "Worst of" list, whether in *Time Magazine*, in *Rolling Stone*, or on *Fox News*.

When I think about the first generation of great female rock singers, the first three names that come to mind are Janis Joplin, Grace Slick, and Joan Baez. I readily admit that any list of female rockers is a short one. After my first three selections, I find myself rationalizing the rest of the list. Don't you?

You probably have your own top three lady rockers that might run the gamut from Tina Turner and Aretha Franklin to Bonnie Raitt, Joan Jett, Deborah Harry, Linda Ronstadt, Stevie Nicks, Joni Mitchell, Judy Collins, Anne Wilson … well, you get the idea.

Janis Joplin and Grace Slick are arguably the alpha and omega of 1970s female rockers, but comparing the Madonna of *Diamonds and Rust* with Janis and Grace takes some major *cojones*. None the less, here I go.

For me, Joan Baez was the counterculture queen during the turbulent days of the 1960s. She was never as original as female songwriters like Joni Mitchell or Carole King, but her interpretations of original material like The Band's "The Night They Drove Old Dixie Down," Paul Simon's "The Boxer," and Phil Ochs' "There But for Fortune Go You And I" were always stunning, vocally impressive, and sincere. She was a political activist who embraced the edgy music of Bob Dylan, marched with Dr. Martin Luther King Jr., and displayed a lifelong commitment to political and social activism.

It was November 15, 1975. Joan Baez was performing at the Niagara Falls Convention Center. The usher who had escorted me to my row ten aisle seat returned to ask if I was Jim Santella. "That's what I'm told," I replied glibly. He gave me a smirk and dropped a bomb on me. "Joan Baez said to bring you backstage."

Oh my God! My request for an interview had been granted.

It was 8:30 p.m. and as I walked backstage, I reminded myself not to ask any questions about Bob Dylan, a good decision that was supported by the road manager's thumbs up gesture to me when two minutes into the interview he gave her a rehearsed gesture and reminder that she needed to get ready. She winked at him and said, "It's okay, I'm having fun." The interview continued for almost fifteen more engaging minutes. I never met Dylan, but I did lose my heart to the "Sad-Eyed Lady of the Lowlands."

The interview remained locked in my memory for decades, but was lost on a misplaced cassette that eventually turned up in my many boxes of memorabilia.

Never throw away artifacts of your past. It is your legacy to your grandchildren when they ask, "What was Grandpa Santella like?" I never really knew either of my maternal or paternal grandfathers. To Marco and Mira, my grandchildren: this is a small part of your legacy. May all of us stay "Forever Young."

What follows are the opinions and classy self-assuredness of the one and only Joan Baez. Make your own judgment.

The following transcription is of an interview with Joan Baez by Jim Santella of Q-FM 97, the local progressive album station in Buffalo, New York. This interview was recorded at about 8:30 p.m. on November 15, 1975, just prior to the second performance in the Niagara Falls Convention Center of the Rolling Thunder Review.

Jim Santella: Did the first performance go well?

Joan Baez: Yes, it went very well. It was what they call "hot." Seems everybody was in good shape.

JS: How did you get involved in the tour? How did it start for you?

JB: Well, Bob called up one night and asked me if I wanted to go on the road.

JS: Simple as that?

JB: Yes. It was simple, because I had already planned to go on the road, so I had that month blocked out for my own tour. The only thing that was un-simple was undoing one month of tours. Within the next forty-eight hours, we were going to sign the contracts. So, fortunately, nothing was signed and I had forty-eight hours to think, to see if it made any sense or not, and for lots of reasons it made sense.

JS: What does this tour mean to you? As a performer, as opposed to other tours you've been on?

JB: Well, the reason I did it was I saw plenty to be gained, lots to be learned, lots of fun to be had. There's a point in my life when I'm not out spearheading campaigns. It hit at really a nice time. It wasn't a time when I felt that I was supposed to be going to jail for one thing or another. I've really eased off that for about a year; I decided to make my priorities with music and family. This seemed great and I was flattered that Bobby asked me.

JS: This tour seems to be an important one, not just for Dylan but for all the people involved. It's not just a bunch of people playing and making money.

Joan Baez, 1975.

PHOTO BY JOHN RIZZO

JB: Bunch of people touring losing money is what it is … (laughter)

JS: What do you do when you are not performing?

JB: Well, you see Bob is all involved in doing a film, and I've done a little bit of that and other people are … involved in that. I get a little bit lost on days off, sometimes. You look around for a sauna or a swimming pool, or you do some music, get together with some people, and jam and make up (songs) or decide on a new song at the next concert.

JS: How set is the performance?

JB: Oh, Christ. It's so un-set. I mean, for instance, when I'm with Bob, the set we do … I never know what he's doing. Today, he said, typically, I asked what are we doing. He said: "The Water's Wide" … plunka/plunka/plunk and then he changed hand positions as I was about to open my mouth and sing and said: "No, let's do 'St. Augustine.'" That's how set it is. Ronee has her part more set and my part with the band is set because I haven't had enough rehearsal time to fluctuate the songs enough. We did try a new one tonight. We tried "Take That Ribbon" ("Help Me Make It Through the Night"); one of those guys was late. [Ed. Note: Mick Ronson was not on stage on time for Joan's first song with the back-up musicians and she gently kidded about being on tour with an English rock star with an impeccable British accent.] That came out nicely, I thought.

JS: What is the relationship as far as growth in doing your early material like "Silver Dagger" through "Long Black Veil" to "Diamonds and Rust"?

JB: You mean the old songs? Well, the way I always looked at that, when I felt myself changing or going in different directions, was that I was not Jean Ritchie. Jean Ritchie is an exquisite presenter of antiques; she displays old traditional songs exactly as they should be sung and she does them beautifully and she'll never change out of that. I did that when I was very young. I did those same songs … I did them as well as I could, but then I felt the need to grow. Bobby felt it before the rest of us and had a whole lot more nerve than I ever had and, you know, picked up the electricity and alienated a lot of people … but … he just has to move … and … I had to move from one thing to another.

JS: The new album [*Diamonds and Rust*] is really doing well for you … it's just recently turned gold.

JB: Yea … [laughter] … I needed that.

JS: I hear that you have some live material that's coming out either this January or February.

JB: Well, we taped last summer's tour.

JS: What are you going to do after that?

JB: I'm going to go home and write a book. I'm about 30,000 words into a book and I'm really anxious to get back to the typewriter. I've been concentrating on that for a while. I can't sing and do that sort of thing at the same time.

JS: Can you give us some idea of what the book is going to be like?

JB: I don't know if you ever saw the little book I wrote called *Daybreak,* but it's experiential stuff, it's about my life, it's all … at this point, I can't write fiction. It's about things that have happened to me or meant something to me and it's in chapters. The one I'm working on now, will probably be the same, only I think there is more in there to be said now, and I think maybe it's a little less mushy. It's nine years later. I found, for instance, that I wrote 20,000 words in one sitting about the bombs in Hanoi that … just came pouring out.

JS: Do you get much flack from your older fans who would like you to be more politically involved? Is this the time … I mean, socially?

JB: I understand … I mean, I haven't taken a break from that for seventeen years, and I had to discipline myself to take a break and not worry about what they were going to say. And I realize, from what good friends who understand me … who were saying, "Well, it's about time that she takes a rest," that they had heard a lot of flack like, "Oh, what is happening to our Joan? She doesn't' care anymore. She's just making money and buying rugs for her house." My first reaction is to say: "Shove it up your ass." And the second one is, well, how would they know that I haven't sold out and decided to just make albums and hang out and let the world go by. I just had to take a rest. My son is at an age where everyone says that in a couple of years I won't have to be with him so much. You don't have to be so careful, but entering first grade and being five years old—they need their mommies around. So, I thought

Photo by Mickey Osterreicher

Joni Mitchell, "Rambling Jack" Elliott, Joan Baez, and Bob Dylan, during the Rolling Thunder Review Tour at the Niagara Falls Convention Center in 1975.

all my rhetoric and all this stuff doesn't mean shit, if I don't bring him up right—if I don't pay proper attention to him. So out of this … there are four of me. There's the mother, the woman, the politician, and the musician. I had to do the music 'cause I was going bankrupt … [laugh] … I wanted to do the mother. I was throwing in a little woman when I can. Now I decided to drop, for the first time in many, many years, to drop the politics, the activism and lay back. But nothing inside me basically had changed … about my fanaticism, about nonviolence, and that's just a given. It's there. I would like to explain it in the book … just a little, maybe. What it means to take a break … how necessary I think it is for people to be allowed to take breaks.

JS: At the risk of being corny, Dylan's line about "The times they are a-changing" seems appropriate. The times are not right for the same devotion ... the atmosphere is different. How can you be doing the same things you were doing in '68 and '69? You have to be doing '75 things. What is the same? How do you maintain your own development or growth?

JB: Well, that's one of the reasons to lay back. When the war … "ended" and the five million people were dead … it sort of was like getting socked in the back of the head. You have to stop and figure out what you are going to do next. I think you have to stop and think. I mean, I did Amnesty International for a full year when I felt the end of that war coming on; then I wanted to be doing the next thing, which was to build up that organization for political prisoners who were being hanged by their heels in Chile, and, oh, thirty countries. I was involved in that. There are things to do, but, as you say, I don't think this is the time to run out in massive demonstrations. There's no handle that's steady enough to grab onto and organize around. Everything is there to be done. Everything is in just as bad a shape as it was two years ago. There isn't that one handle—which was Vietnam—that everyone was desperately working on. You know … people that were interested in that thing … Cesar Chavez, in a sense, is the only viable nonviolent organization to throw yourself into. There are the people who are very interested in exposing the CIA. There are things like that going on, that are good.

JS: Does it seem that more things are being worked out through the system? Instead of overt demonstrations and the tearing down of the organized walls of the system, it seems that more things are coming from out of the government, of young politicians, out of a whole consciousness that may have been raised in the whole country, even in old people. The moment seems to arise more through the established people and methods of the government.

JB: You mean through the system?

JS: Yes. It seems that more is being accomplished through the system.

JB: I don't know. It all depends on what, in the end, can be accomplished. You are kind of narrowing it down to saying that people … like say my ex-husband running for Congress. I mean, he is saying things that two years ago he would never have said. He has to, to get it on the brochure. He absolutely has to … he has to … instead of saying, "I will never again fight in a war," he has to say, "I will never support an unjust war." Aaagh! I hate it. I love him. He's on the side of the angels, and I think he'll do good things. If he gets in there, he'll do them anyway. The one reason I would want him to be in Congress is that he has the background. He was in jail … he knows something … he knows what's going on with those people … he knows the underground of America. But, aside from that, I'm very uncomfortable talking about changes coming about through the system, because the system is the Nation-State. There's no way to drag those two apart. And my feeling is that it's the Nation-State that is snuffing out human beings. The reason that we fight and slaughter each other and all the young boys, eighteen-to-something-or-other, die or get their arms blown off and become quadriplegics is because the nation is more important than the human being … And being part of that system, you pledge your allegiance to that Nation-State. There's no way around it; it's going to be very hard for David or Tom Hayden.

JS: Then there's almost a hypocrisy … or contradiction between the two [managers enter to tell Joan that the interview should end as performance time is near. Joan is very polite and grants additional time.]

JB: [In response to manager's motions] Take another five minutes 'cause it's interesting.

JS: Can I ask you just one more thing about music? Would you comment about performing alone on a stool by yourself, as opposed to performing with a band as on *Diamonds and Rust*?

JB: Performing by myself gives a lot more freedom of what to choose—a song, or change a word, or whatever. Performing with a band is more musical freedom. You can depend upon them for the parts that I would otherwise be filling in. I am not that much of a guitarist. I am absolutely adequate for everything that I do. I'm careful with it, but I'm not a virtuoso. If I have adequate backing it's more fun, or, I should say, it can be a lot more fun.

JS: I was impressed with you on the *Midnight Special*.

JB: Oh! I was a corpse on the *Midnight Special*.

JS: No, not the show you were on, the tribute to you, the clips.

JB: I didn't see those.

JS: I loved them. I'd forgotten about Joan Baez. Joan Baez was still the person I was in college that I rallied around and all of that. [Profuse blushing by professional radio broadcaster.] The reason

I asked about the band was that I loved seeing you by yourself. I thought you were so much at ease ... and I didn't care what you sang. It was so enjoyable just seeing you, and when you sang it was just perfect ... all those elements. That's why I asked if you enjoyed performing more with the band or by yourself.

JB: Well, in something like this, I am completely cramped. It's not my show. It's somebody else's show and I've been given more minutes than anybody else except the principal ... [Manager: "Five 'til show."] ... O.K. So I do what I can without it. It's a very different thing than having your own two-hour show where I can do whatever I want, depending on how the mood dictates, and do political stuff, nonpolitical stuff, funny, imitations, anything. If I do go out with a band, I do half the stuff alone and half the stuff with them ... to cover all the bases ... to cover my own and everyone else's, and when I do my acoustic set, that's when I say things or sing "Sacco-Vanzetti," or I'll talk about political prisoners or I'll mention farm workers. All that freedom that I don't have here. There's no way to have that freedom on someone else's show. Not only their show but it's a rock 'n' roll show. Except for Jack Elliott and myself.

JS: Thank you very much.

Not only is Joan Baez an extremely talented performer, whether singing or just relating to an audience as an entertainer, when she smiles at you, it is warm, genuine, and extremely gracious. Walking away from an interview with Joan Baez, you feel as though you have not only had the privilege of being with a sensitive performer but that you have also had the opportunity to share in the experiences of a rare person, a person who leaves a mark upon you as a human, caring individual. You leave with the gift of her insight. Our conversation transcended opinions and reflected the strength of her honest beliefs.

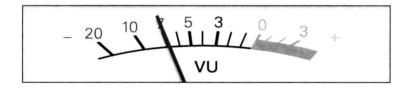

SEVEN

A New Lease on Life

I left for Woodstock with few expectations and returned to Buffalo enlightened. Like any modern creation story, Woodstock's Children of God created a mythical Eden. While God needed seven days to create the universe, the Woodstock Nation used only four to create its own appropriate miracles, delivered by apostles with names like Chip Monk and the Hog Farm's Wavy Gravy who turned meager loaves of bread into shared food, drink, and drugs. During those four days, we left the world behind and found peace inside this bubble of a new universe. Forever after, people would ask: "Were you there?"

As John, Bernie, Sir Walter, and I walked back to our car, the realization that we were returning to the real world began to seep in. Driving home we discussed everything we had seen and experienced; none of us had a good handle on it yet. More than four decades later, I still don't. Despite having experienced the event of the century, at the time it was just four guys with dirty clothes heading home.

For me Woodstock was not the end of a monumental event but the beginning of a four-decade-long radio career. Upon leaving Woodstock, I began to further develop personal programming ideas that would last me a lifetime. It started with a phone call.

I got back to Buffalo at noon and within two hours received a call from WYSL-FM's program director, Paul Palo, who had been calling me all weekend. Now there's a story. He offered me my job back. Within the last few days a couple of disc jockeys had been caught with some marijuana stashed away in the music library. Three jocks were fired. Yes, they needed someone, and they needed someone right away. Wow! That adage is true: you'll never work in this town again ... unless we need you! It was almost September, and, once again, I was working in commercial radio. If Woodstock was a treasure, being rehired by WYSL-FM was like finding a gold mine.

I had gotten the job of a lifetime, gotten fired from the job of a lifetime, experienced the event of a lifetime, and gotten rehired, all within eight months. My guardian angel was working overtime.

BITS AND PIECES

For the next three years, I held the 10 p.m. to 2 a.m. shift at WYSL-FM 103.3. The station was now broadcasting twenty-four/seven, no longer simulcasting with the AM station during the day. To further distance us from the AM station's Top 40 format, our call letters were changed to WPHD-FM in January 1970. Contrary to popular opinion, WLSD was never considered as the new station call letters. The decision was made at corporate headquarters in Dallas and we were never consulted. Makes a good story though.

Many DJs went through that station and moved on quickly. The turn-over included Sir Walter Raleigh, Harold Turner, Clyde Collins, H. F. Stone, Jeff Lubeck, as well as my good friend Al Wallack, an important jazz programmer in Buffalo radio, host of *Jazz in the Nighttime*.

I wish I could remember all the events that occurred then, and all of the musicians who came into the WPHD studio to be interviewed, but, to be honest, one cool event melded into the next, so now they are just bits and pieces of my radio life. Now when I reminisce with friends and fans, these events seem iconic, but as I was living them, it was hard to gauge their significance, except for the fact that it all felt special.

How do you explain meeting musicians like Dr. John, The Band, Joni Mitchell, Steve Winwood and Traffic, Keith Emerson, The Moody Blues, Genesis, and Alice Cooper? From the world of the blues, I met B. B. King, Muddy Waters, Little Walter, Buddy Guy, and John Lee Hooker. The list is endless. Back then, musicians would speak to DJs, there wasn't such a disconnect between the artists and radio personalities. I never knew who would show up with an ambitious promo man. That all changed around 1975 when underground radio morphed into Lee Abrams' SuperStars format. Nowadays, superstars don't do radio station interviews. But more about that later.

At this time, four of my favorite musicians were Lowell George from Little Feat, Donald Fagen and Walter Becker from Steely Dan, and the ubiquitous Frank Zappa. I got to interview all of them.

I remember Frank Zappa telling me about his appearance on *The Tonight Show* with Steve Allen. I asked him if this was before he formed his alter ego, the Mothers of Invention. He said, "Oh yes. I was in my '50s doo-wop phase. However, what got me on the show was telling the producer I was a composer and I played exotic instruments like the bicycle." I looked at him in disbelief. Making music with a pair of drumsticks and a bicycle was pure Frank Zappa. Many years later, I saw the clip on YouTube. It is hilarious.

Walter Becker and Donald Fagen, who named their band after a dildo in William Burrough's *The Naked Lunch*, utilized some of the most creative studio musicians to define their sound. Becker, who answered most of my questions, explained how they would frequently begin a song with an eclectic lyric or musical phrase and then invite top Los Angeles jazz and rock musicians to layer solos on top of their musical ideas. No matter who eventually was selected to play, it always resulted in the "Steely Dan sound." Fagen summed it up best when he concluded that they never knew what their music would be until the final mix.

When I interviewed Lowell George, he held onto his unplugged electric guitar throughout the entire interview, silently playing a tune between answers to my questions. I ended up paying more attention to his fingers than to the answers he gave. I wish I could have heard what he was hearing.

What characterized all four of these musicians was intelligence, a unique vision of their music, and a sense of humor. Ultimately, it revealed more about my values than their gifts.

When I interviewed Jerry Garcia at Kleinhans, he disappointed me with his crass remarks and gestures. The next time I saw him was equally negative. I was backstage at Shea's and saw him snub one of the ardent Deadheads that the band routinely attracted. Over the years, I have mellowed my opinion about that rudeness, though. Rock stars are constantly being bombarded with love and affection by their fans. What starts out as ego-inflating devotion turns into privacy-invading demands from acolytes. It must be difficult to be a god. Years later, listening to a bootleg copy of the July 4, 1989, Rich Stadium concert, I realized how good the Dead were. Perhaps my opinion about them had been colored by my Garcia encounters.

GUITAR WORKSHOP

Around this time I thought it would be fun, and easy, to learn to play the guitar. After all, how difficult could it be to learn three chords and play rock, blues, or folk music? Jimi Hendrix, Stevie Ray Vaughn, and Duane Allman notwithstanding, wasn't most popular music rather simple? Armed with that wayward notion, I bought an acoustic Epiphone guitar and an Artie Traum lesson book. The fact that it was an advanced instruction book did nothing to deter my enthusiasm.

Two weeks later, I was still struggling to hold the strings down on the one chord I knew—E Major. When I complained on the air about my frustration, I got a call from Jerry Raven, a local folk guitarist and singer/songwriter. He volunteered to give me a few free lessons. I was elated. We planned to meet the next Saturday at a deserted storefront on the corner of Franklin and Virginia. The night before the lesson, I mentioned my good fortune on the air and invited any amateur guitarist to come join us. Since I didn't expect more than two or three people to show up, I didn't mention anything to Jerry. Imagine my surprise when over thirty bodies with guitars showed up. Jerry took it in stride. It was the beginning of the Guitar Workshop. It lasted only a year but it was great fun. I remained friends with some of those people for life, like Buffalo State College professor Diane McFarland. More than a few of the group went on to play professionally. I wasn't one of them!

Events like my interview with Garcia were balanced by my interview with singer/songwriter Jackson Browne, who performed at UB and later spent two full hours with me on the air. Afterwards, we headed out for breakfast at the Towne Restaurant, Browne's treat. He was a genuinely friendly guy, easy to talk with and a talented songwriter. He came back six months later a full-blown star, and "Doctor My Eyes" was at the top of the charts. Our relationship changed, and his accessibility was greatly reduced.

Bonnie Raitt, with her blazing red hair, dimples, and freckles, was a lot of fun. She and I also had lunch together at the Towne Restaurant before her concert. I loved her Koko Taylor-like bluesy voice and great smile. She told me about her college days with Faye Dunaway and how they'd spend more time partying than in class. My kind of woman. Only when her dad, Broadway star John Raitt, came to visit did they dress "properly," wearing nice dresses and shoes, and act like good students.

After an Eagle's concert, singer Don Henley and I spent almost three hours in a conversation about spirituality, and a week later he gave me a gift of three books on Zen Buddhism. Talk about Zen moments!

I once heard a college student talking to Fito de la Parra, drummer for Canned Heat, about spurring on the revolution. Fito said something like: "Okay. You got the guns?" The student looked bewildered. "When you get the guns, call me and we'll get that revolution going." Fito winked at me.

IN THE STUDIO

On the air our listeners loved the tintinnabulation of chimes underneath the DJ's voice. Decades later, people still ask me about them. Here's the skinny on the chimes: They were not live, but chimes recorded on an endless loop. We were always coming up with little gimmicks like that to spring on the audience.

Our tiny studio on the eighteenth floor of the Hotel Statler in downtown Buffalo was a small corner office, with shelves of records, a

Our cramped WYSL-FM studio on the eighteenth floor of the Hotel Statler in 1970. No expense was spared.

few artificial plants, two record players, one table, a broadcast board, and a microphone. How small was it? The studio mice were hunchbacked! (Rim shot!) Sometimes I could actually hear the rodents scurrying through the record shelves when I was on the air. "And that's the truth!" In fact, it was during an attempt to trap some mice that management found the illicit drugs in the record shelves.

The studio mice were positively friendly compared to walking the gauntlet of the hotel lobby, though. It was a study in contrasts:

businessmen with their suits and briefcases, guests in their travel finery, and the hippie-dippie DJs. For me, it was not fun. I had a long beard, cowboy hat, and peace symbol belt buckle. Not only was I given snooty looks, people were bold enough to talk about me in the third person, as if I didn't exist. Once I entered the elevator with an elderly couple and the woman loudly asked her husband: "Why are people like him in this hotel?" I made a lame remark about his mother and moved on. Sometimes, the hotel staff would stop me as I walked by and ask: "Excuse me. Can I help you?" as if I didn't belong there. I'd reply, "I work here." Sometimes I wish my mother hadn't given me such good manners.

By the end of 1970, WYSL-AM and WPHD-FM had moved to new studios at 325 Franklin Street. The FM studio was even smaller than the one at the Statler. It felt like home there, though. Thankfully the mice did not move with us. It was just the AM jocks we had to contend with. Sometimes we felt like Rodney Dangerfield: We didn't get any respect!

We never knew who would come through the studio doors in that place. One night, shortly after midnight, a musician named James Peterson brought his five-year-old son to see me and tried to get me to play a new record his son had recorded. James owned the Governor's Inn, a local blues club. I was polite but noncommittal. As it turned out, the young lad falling asleep in his dad's arms was Lucky Peterson, who grew up to be a famous Buffalo blues musician. Months later, the song, "1,2,3,4" hit the national Top 40 charts, and he appeared on *The Tonight Show*.

THE UB RIOTS

I still cry when I think of the May 4, 1970, shootings at Kent State. College campuses were alive with student protests against the war in Vietnam and the draft. In the spring of that year, before the Kent State shootings, student protests at UB came to a head. I was there the day the police stormed the campus. It was an emotional and philosophical turning point for me. Up until then, I think I was just a weekend radical. My friend Ann Sterling and I would attend Students for a Democratic Society (SDS) and Youth Against War and Fascism (YAWF) meetings. They were radical left organizations. We participated in weekend anti-war protests held in Niagara Square. I still have a memory of FBI agents in their black suits and brown shoes taking pictures of the demonstrators. They were so obvious, it was like a scene out of *Men in Black*. Ann would even call out to some of them by name. I'm sure there's an FBI folder on me somewhere.

I spent most of my spare time at WBFO where the student staff had the opportunity to cover the riots. They had much better access to the demonstrators than other local media. Lengthy interviews with undergrad and grad students, along with professors, made coverage appear to be all protest, all the time. Instructors even canceled classes so that students could get together and discuss the war and current events at Teach-Ins.

The riot experience made me a full-blown radical. The whole incident began peacefully, with students staging a sit-in at the Student Union and a few hundred protesters outside. Student photographers, like Mickey Osterreicher, captured many of the events on film. Police in full riot gear ringed the campus. At first I was just an observer, watching the students and the police, who had by now surrounded the campus. Suddenly, I heard a policeman call my name: "Hey, Santella! Get out of here. Go home!" It was my uncle, George Lobuzzetta, warning me. He knew there was going to be trouble and wanted to protect me. I began to head home, just blocks away, but turned around and went back to the Union.

The Vietnam War protests turned into riots on the UB Main Street campus in 1972.

I was too naïve to understand that I was on a collision course with the Buffalo police.

At some point they moved from the perimeter and onto the campus grounds. Students taunted them. All of a sudden, police stormed the Union and started chasing us out. No longer just an observer, I ran out with them. Police were lobbing canisters of eye-searing tear gas and wielding batons. It really got frightening. The sharpest memory I have is getting that tear gas in my eyes and how much it stung. It was my first encounter with the chemical. It wasn't pleasant. I don't remember how I got out of there, but this time I heeded Uncle George's advice and went home.

For the next two weeks I practically lived on campus, hanging out at the radio station. I saw broken glass doors, burned-out trash barrels, and policemen arresting students and dragging them off the campus. It was the closest I'd ever been to police brutality. Shortly afterward, the massacre at Kent State reinforced the terror of the times.

JONI MITCHELL

One of my favorite colors is yellow. I have Joni Mitchell to thank for that. I had fallen in love with folk music, especially blue grass, blues, and fiddle tunes. I struggled mightily with my brand new Epiphone guitar, to no avail. Hearing that the Mariposa Folk Festival at Toronto's Centre Island had workshops that showcased unpretentious performers like Doc Watson, the Holy Modal Rounders, Elizabeth Cotton, David Bromberg, and even Muddy Waters, I decided to make the ninety-mile or so trip to Toronto. I stayed for three days, attended a bunch of workshops and learned to absolutely love the color yellow. You see, Joni Mitchell made an appearance on the main stage.

I was familiar with her work, but I had mixed feelings about her talent. Her songs were innovative, poetic, and emotional but her quirky voice bothered me. It was a hot summer day as I took my seat on one of the hard wooden chairs set up on the lawn. A five-word introduction, "Ladies and gentlemen, Joni Mitchell," preceded her appearance in a deeply hued, long yellow summer dress. It outshone the sun. I couldn't take my eyes off of her. Joni is not pretty in the same way as Judy Collins or Joan Baez, but she is commanding in her ability to transform songs, delivery, and creativity into a universe of emotion. The memory of that performance is blurred by the passage of time, but the vision of that yellow dress is forever etched in my memory.

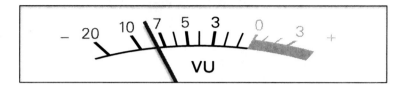

EIGHT

Programming Is My Passion

The one thing I was allowed, no matter which station I worked at, was freedom. I treasured the freedom to program my shows by instinct, without interference. Programming music, especially for an underground station, meant that you played a lot of music that didn't normally get heard. You had to present it in a more audience-friendly manner than formatted radio stations that used the repetition of Billboard-dominated charts as a template.

This is important because AM radio glorified the single. FM radio, from *Sgt. Pepper's* on, used the concept of the unified LP for song choices. Top 40 radio programmed the same thirty to forty best-selling songs repeated endlessly with a few "oldies" and "new releases" thrown in for variety. They'd wear out the 45s. Album-Oriented Radio operated with twenty- to thirty-minute sets of uninterrupted music. Instead of using sales or popularity to choose songs, I developed thematic building blocks of music that provided variety, unity, and challenged the audience. Hell, that was the FM DJ's stock in trade. Thematic blocks of music became my passion.

BUILDING TOWERS OF SOUND

I played sets of music that appeared to be very atypical if you looked at just the list of artists. I linked songs together by theme, by subject, by related artists, or I could just put my hand on the record shelf and

HOW TO BE A CREATIVE DISC JOCKEY

First: a little preparation goes a long way. Of course, you could randomly grab a stack of disks, drop the needle or play all of your favorites and get by with, "That was … This is … Coming up next …" But that is not freeform radio. It's radio by the numbers.

Most of what you need to say on air fits on 3x5 cards. I've taught students how to be a jock in five minutes (wink, wink, nudge, nudge). Just try the following exercise. I guarantee you will need less than five minutes to master it. On five 3x5 cards write out:

> Card 1: Your name
> Card 2: Station Call Letters
> Card 3: Name of Song
> Card 4: Time & Temperature
> Card 5: Next Song

Now read the cards in all possible combinations: 12345, 23451, 34521, 45123, etc. Do the math and you'll see there are 120 possible variations before you repeat one. Try it. Some combinations will sound better than others, but all will work. Here's how it goes.

> 12345:
> "Jim Santella on WUWU with 'Free Bird.' It's 9:50 a.m. and seventy-six degrees. Here's 'Stairway to Heaven.'"

Very lean and telegraphic, but organized and easy to deliver confidently—inexperienced DJs generally talk too much and don't say anything. After you master that model, it's time to add a little personality.

> "I'm Jim Santella, and you know who you are. If you just tuned into WUWU, the bad news is you missed "Free Bird,' one of the legendary rock anthems that has defined a generation of baby boomers. It's 9:50 and seventy-six sunny degrees. The good news is, I have another rock anthem for you. The elevator is broken and you will have to take the 'Stairway to Heaven.'"

pull out something weird like "Ogdens' Nut Gone Flake" by the Small Faces. There were so many possibilities. I was connecting things in my own way, like a musical puzzle I was solving. And the audience had to make that connection. Why were these songs being played together? What was the common thread? In reality, most audience members just enjoyed the variety of music being played and only sometimes saw the connection. Regardless, they knew they liked it.

FM radio tended to make musical, political, or social statements. For instance, The Byrds' "Turn, Turn, Turn," Buffalo Springfield's "For What It's Worth," "Mr. Soul" by Neil Young, and The Hollies' "Bus Stop" could be enjoyed as four separate songs. They could also be recognized as the solo work of Crosby, Stills, Nash, and Young. Thematically, they explored subjects as varied as the Bible, rebellion, racism, and summer love. FM radio was providing a point of view not available on AM radio.

I loved building towers of music. I never claimed to be the first jock to put a set of songs together thematically, but it was my preferred programming style. It created a total fabric of subject, sound, and statement, and I was good at it. Imagination, an encyclopedic knowledge of music, and a huge music library helped me pull it off.

It's one thing to play a song you like, whether the appeal is the words, beat, voice, or style, but to weave all of those qualities together, and then some, is music programming taken to the level of art. A good example would be exploring songs about horses: "A Horse with No Name," "Wild Horses," "One Trick Pony," "Chestnut Mare," and "Heavy Horses." The result provided more than the sum of the individual parts. Remember all those "compare and contrast" college essays? I enjoyed doing that with my play list.

I liked spotlighting homegrown talent. For example, I would play a local set with Gary Mallaber, who played with Van Morrison; Dick Kermode, heard with Janis Joplin and Carlos Santana; Sandi Konikoff, who played on the Joe Cocker live album *Mad Dogs and Englishmen*; and a Billy Sheehan tune he played with David Lee Roth. The talent in Buffalo was world class. They were all well-known Buffalo musicians who went on to gain a national reputation. The bands Raven and later Talas would also fit in a local set.

Getting into and out of a song is also important. "Back in the USSR" by the Beatles can be followed by Steve Miller's "Jet Airliner." Both songs are audience favorites, but playing them back-to-back brings attention to airplane travel or life on the road or homesickness or the Cold War.

The Beatles' song alone is packed with a musical gumbo of themes and statements from Chuck Berry's "Back in the USA" to Beach Boys harmonies.

There's also what I call copycat song selection. Just play a song set of the same tune: for example, begin with the original acoustic version of "Dust My Broom" by Robert Johnson and then play Eric Clapton's version recorded three decades later.

Another technique is to move from one song to another within the same style. I could play an Allman Brothers song followed by a Lynard Skynard song. Both groups play blues rock. The bands don't sound alike, but they have similar qualities that go together well.

Beginnings, endings, and nonmusical elements also make great transitions. I would use sound effects found on the record itself to cross-fade songs together. The Beatles have that jet whoosh sound at the beginning and the end of "Back in the U.S.S.R." You can whoosh right into another song with a similar effect, like "Fly Like an Eagle" by the Steve Miller Band. You can do the same thing with drum beats. I might make a long cross-fade with the end of one song over the beginning of the next, so that the casual listener couldn't tell where one ended and the other began.

The shift in music from the pop-oriented single to the much deeper album format was reflected in the radio personalities as well. DJs had always been, first and foremost, entertainers. It was no longer enough to come on the air, full of energy, to just dedicate and introduce the next single. Listeners wanted more.

For me, the best radio people have been able to combine fun, music, and intelligence. I worked with the late AM jock Don Berns at WPHD-FM during its final six months and fell prey to his infectious laugh and good-natured musical knowledge. My two favorite FM jocks, however, were both Canadian: Reiner Swartz and David Pritchard, both of CHUM-FM. They were adventurous rascals who taught me more than a little bit about putting together music and ideas. Pritchard stretched vowels until they broke under the strain of carrying too heavy a load. Then he'd play some esoteric group with a name like Tonto's Expanding Headband and I'd nearly drive off the road laughing.

Here's a summary of some of the key differences between FM and AM radio programming during the 1960s and 1970s:

AM RADIO vs. FM RADIO

Played short singles	Played long album tracks
Jocks followed a playlist	Jocks picked the music
Loud entertainment	Conversational and laid-back
Humor driven	Talked about music
Hit driven	Progressive and political
Teeny bopper audience	Students and hippies
Jingles separated cuts	Three-song segues
Music as entertainment	Music as art
Teenage themes	Adult lyrics
Self-centered	Social revolution
Singles	Albums treated as single
AM radio had a noisy signal	FM radio signal was noisefree

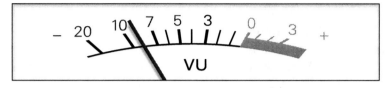

NINE

Small Venue Concerts versus Arena Concerts

My first live concert was like my first kiss: irrepressible, singular, heady, and impossible to explain. Her name was Tootsie Hale. We were both four. I don't remember any more details.

My first live concert, on the other hand, was nothing but details. I was thirteen and it was held at Kleinhans Music Hall, located a block and a half from my house at 103 Plymouth Avenue on Buffalo's West Side. Like Goldilocks, I've always considered Kleinhans to be the perfect size venue. Not too big, not too small. Just right.

The concert was called *Jazz for Moderns* and was hipper than hip. (I still have the program.) The Chico Hamilton Quintet featured a jazz cellist and Chico's drumming highlighted by his mesmerizing mallet work. Blind British pianist George Shearing's quartet featured a lady vibraphonist and a cool blend of standards and originals. Shearing was quite the showman in his dark sunglasses and ebullient style. He even had the audacity to do a spot-on imitation of Ray Charles, which brought down the house. Baritone saxophonist Gerry Mulligan's quintet stopped after playing only a few notes. Mulligan addressed the sound technician, directing him to turn off the sound system. "This hall doesn't need any amplification. It's perfect." It was the ultimate tribute to Finnish architects Eliel and Eero Saarinen's acoustically perfect hall. And with that accolade, he launched into "Line for Lyons," his bebop standard written for West Coast jazz DJ Jimmy Lyons.

I was in bebop heaven. Yes, I was a jazz-bo even at the tender age of thirteen. My musical taste always seemed to extend beyond the expected. While still in my teens, I heard jazz giants like Miles Davis at Kleinhans and John Coltrane at the legendary Royal Arms on West Utica Street. During intermission, Coltrane actually went backstage and practiced scales for twenty minutes, and then came back out for his second set. It was such a small club that Coltrane played on top of the circular bar. Intimate venues like these brought you into the music with an emphasis on up close and personal. I was underage, but no one seemed to notice or care.

SMALL VENUES

In those early, heady days of FM radio, concerts occurred at small venues and clubs. For me, these were the best places to enjoy live music. Kleinhans, with about three thousand seats, featured rock groups like The Who (November 15, 1969) and Frank Zappa and The Mothers of Invention who shared the stage with Flo & Eddie (The Turtles) on October 23, 1970. Yes, Virginia, rock music was booked at Kleinhans. Rock has reigned in Buffalo since that time.

It wasn't unusual for two and sometimes three "name" bands to perform at Kleinhans on a single evening. Remember, this was back in the days before arena rock concerts dominated. I remember seeing Alvin Lee, the New York Dolls, and Ten Years After, all on the same bill. That night, I was backstage ready to introduce the glam rock New York Dolls and suddenly a fist whistled past my ear—a fight had broken out between vocalist David Johansen and guitarist Johnny Thunder. A couple of roadies separated them. I introduced the quarreling musicians and they went on stage as if nothing had happened. It was one of my first encounters with the New York punk scene which, at that time, was dominated by The Velvet Underground. I loved their version of "White Light, White Heat." Years later, I got to see Lou Reed at Shea's right after the release of his *Transfomer* album. One overly enthusiastic fan jumped up on the stage and tackled him with a huge hug.

The Tralf and Stage One only held about four hundred people each. But they were bigger than the small clubs, like those on the Hertel Strip, from the Bona Vista to Aliotta's Lounge. On April 29, 1970, it got a little

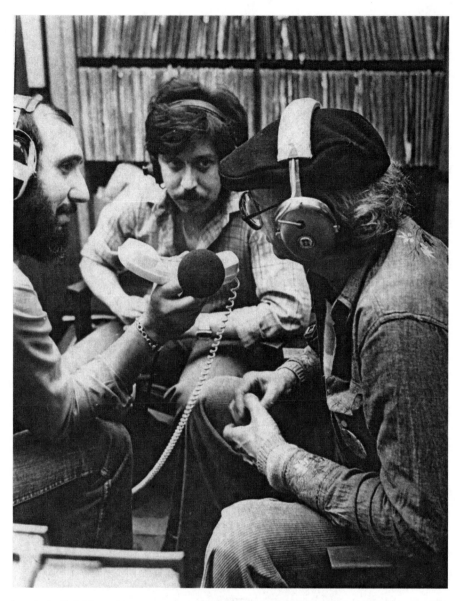

Interviewing Buffalo's premier concert promoters, Harvey and Corky's Eddy Tice, and Jerry Nathan of Festival East.

too up close and personal at Aliotta's when the Allman Brothers band, with guitar genius Duane Allman prior to their big breakout, rocked the joint. They had taken the long jaunt from Jacksonville to introduce southern fried blues to Buffalo, playing classic blues like "One Way Out," "Must Have Done Somebody Wrong," and "Statesboro Blues."

I was at Aliotta's that night. After the concert, the owner was stabbed to death by Twigs, the Allman Brothers' road manager, in an argument about the band's pay. Lucky for me, I had left an hour earlier.

In the missed concert column, I passed up the opportunity to see Elvis perform on April 5, 1972, at Memorial Auditorium. In hindsight, it was like declining an invitation to the Last Supper.

It was a time when Harvey & Corky Productions and Festival East were fledgling entrepreneurs. When Jerry Nathan ran Festival East, he brought in jazz groups. When his son, David Nathan, took over, he booked rock groups. If you saw a rock concert in the 1970s in Buffalo, odds are the band was brought in by one of these two concert promoters.

Harvey Weinstein was not a big movie mogul then. Harvey, his brother Bob, and Corky Burger, formed Harvey & Corky Productions. Weinstein got his promoting experience working as music chairman for UB's student council. Never known for his sweet disposition, he was one of the early maverick promoters who took chances, cut corners, and made Buffalo important on the rock 'n' roll circuit. I was there when they booked their early concerts. I emceed many of them, but I also had the unfortunate distinction of coming face-to-face with Harvey's monumental wrath.

I got along with Weinstein as well as anyone, meaning just barely. When he first acquired the Century Theater, he wrote a three-page letter of welcome to the audience, promising the moon. I was the emcee and he expected me to read it. Rock audiences never suffer fools or long-winded disc jockeys lightly. I condensed Weinstein's expansive speech and brought the band out to a huge yell of approval. Weinstein followed me from the stage to the mezzanine, accusing me of sabotaging his opening. The air was filled with four-letter words and the threat of never introducing another of his rock concerts. It was another instance of "You'll never work in this town again! ... unless I need you." It took only three years before I introduced another band at a Harvey & Corky-sponsored event. He later hired me as house DJ at his rock club, Stage One. See what I mean about luck?

There were times when I was at a particular place, saw a particular band, and it just stayed with me. In 1973, I saw the jazz fusion Mahavishnu Orchestra at the Century and, let me tell you, when they came out, they came out smokin'. It was just exhilarating. They didn't let down for one minute. That was the best live concert I ever saw by the Mahavishnu Orchestra.

For someone like me, who has been afraid of water all of his life, concerts at the Hardrock Quarry in Clarence were a mixed blessing. I loved the music, but I kept the lifeguards nearby, even when I was nowhere near the deep end! The quarry couldn't have had a better name; hard rock bands like Savoy Brown, The Guess Who, and Wishbone Ash all made appearances there in the summer of 1973. Eight hours of sunshine, swimming, and loud music produced wicked sunburns and incipient hearing loss in many of us who now wear hearing aids.

On January 9, 1969, two great events happened concurrently. On the West Coast, Led Zeppelin started their first American tour, headlining Bill Graham's Fillmore West. On the East Coast, WYSL-FM signed on the air as Buffalo's first progressive radio station, and I went on the air with "Sunshine of Your Love." Nine short months later, in October 1969, Led Zeppelin performed at Kleinhans, opening with "Communication Breakdown" played at ear-splitting volume. "Dazed and Confused" left me in precisely that condition.

How was I able to go to so many concerts? Comps. Working in radio, I got complimentary tickets all the time. I was spoiled. To this day, it still seems strange to pay for a concert ticket. But I do support local bands. I've seen more than my fair share of legends, loonies, and ultimate concerts. Here's a short list: B.B. King, John Lee Hooker, Howling Wolf, James Cotton, Buddy Guy, Junior Wells, Lennon, Hendrix, Clapton, Beck, Page, Zappa, Zeppelin, Johnny Winter, ZZ Top, Genesis, ELP, ELO, Pink Floyd, The Moody Blues, King Crimson, the Stones, the Kinks, the Ramones, Bob Dylan, Joan Baez, the Sex Pistols … and the beat goes on.

As a music reviewer from the 1970s through the 2000s, I heard hundreds of groups. Some were already famous when I saw them; some went on to fame, like Buffalo's own Goo Goo Dolls, Ani DiFranco, and 10,000 Maniacs, and some slipped into obscurity. There are too many to remember, but the top drawer of my bedroom dresser is still filled to overflowing with ticket stubs. One thing I can say about all the concerts I've seen: my best concert memories are almost always of those that took place in small, intimate venues.

Bluesmen

Y ou'd be surprised at what can and does happen at concerts. It seems the bigger the performer the more explosive an event can become. Unexpected behavior can spring up out of the blue. Being backstage at any concert is always a tsunami of clashing egos, edgy talent, and boiling energy in search of the perfect marriage between the performers' and audiences' needs.

HOWLIN' WOLF

Blues legends can be pugnacious. "Hey Junior, where'd you get those tight-ass pants?" Howlin' Wolf's booming voice barked out insults at Junior Wells like a champion bowler on his way to a 300 game. Thus started a lengthy verbal joust between a tipsy Howlin' Wolf (Chester Burnette) and a deferential Junior Wells (Amos Blakemore Jr.), two of Chicago blues' most distinctive voices.

I saw both of them for the first time in 1968 at an outdoor blues concert at the University at Buffalo. In the blues world, they didn't come much bigger than Howlin' Wolf. At 300 pounds, the Mississippi Delta native, dressed in bib coveralls, dominated blues clubs and festivals around the world. When the spirit moved him, the country blues performer would crawl across the stage on his hands and knees while howling at the moon. On the other hand, the much younger Junior Wells weighed in at a puny 135 pounds, less than half the weight of Howlin' Wolf. At this time, Wells was just coming into his own as a formidable urban blues player.

On this day, Howlin' Wolf was more than just big, he was intimidating. He entered the backstage area in high dudgeon, aiming his verbal barbs at Junior Wells. Wolf was noted for his world-class temper. Emceeing the event, I viewed up close and dangerous the sparring match between the two. Standing between them in the backstage tent area, I felt like a pickle in the middle.

It wasn't only the Chicago-style blues they played that connected these master bluesmen, but the enormous amount of alcohol they had consumed over the course of the concert. Howlin' Wolf lost no time in opening his guitar case and pulling out a flask of Old Crow. He had come to the backstage area well before start time and by concert time had made quite a dent in the flask. For some unknown reason, he took the opportunity to pick on the dapper Junior Wells' tight-fitting black pants, and continued to do so for the entire concert.

The situation was not helped by the fact that a young college student was interviewing Junior, and not Howlin' Wolf, for the school newspaper. The student was talking to Junior like a genuine fan, naming albums and asking questions. "You tell him, Junior" and "You tell him how to play the blues," bellowed Wolf. The mixture was volcanic.

Howlin' Wolf saw the incongruity between his baggy overalls and Wells's form-fitting pants, thus the pointed barb: "Hey Junior! Where'd you get those tight-ass pants?" Had anyone else talked to Junior like that, he probably would have responded in kind, but the deferential Wells said nothing. My job: to make sure the two performers didn't break each other's neck. It got to be mighty testy out there. As Wolf took more and more sips from his flask, the playful joshing became more and more prickly. In hindsight, I realize that Wolf was performing, not just for Junior, but for all of the other blues performers present—guitarist Buddy Guy, harmonica virtuoso Little Walter, bassist and composer Willie Dixon, pianist Pine-Top Perkins, guitarist Hubert Sumlin, and drummer Fred Belew. He wanted everyone to know he was still the cock of the walk!

Eventually, music prevailed, though. Once the music started, the shenanigans subsided. When Howlin' Wolf took the stage, there was no doubt who the legendary blues performer was. After his set, he ended the evening by putting his arm around Junior Wells. Go figure!

PROFESSOR LONGHAIR AND NEW ORLEANS BLUES

My very first encounter with New Orleans-style blues included Fats Domino, dinner with his music director, Dave Bartholomew, and Professor Longhair, who spoke to me from the porch of his 9th Ward home.

When I was in college in the mid-1960s, I became enamored of the piano stylings and sound of Professor Longhair ("Roy" Byrd), a New Orleans pianist. I was so into his music that I decided to take a week off of school, travel to New Orleans, and look him up. After connecting with each other by phone, I found the Professor in his small, unassuming home. I was surprised at how opposite he was from Howlin' Wolf. He was very slight and, although formal at first, he later warmed up. He was only about fifty years old when I met him. He seemed much older. At first the Professor was more interested in keeping an eye on his teenaged niece than he was in talking to me. She was flirting with the boy next door. 'Fess was none too happy with her behavior, and he let her know it.

Professor Long Hair
Phone 947-3215 · New Orleans, La.

I was invited onto the Professor's porch. It was a porch, mind you, not a veranda. He offered me a glass of iced tea, but I secretly wished to share a real drink with him. He certainly was a contrast to Howlin' Wolf in that respect, too. My first question turned into my last question. No matter what I tried to ask him, he answered everything with, "They stole my music." He wanted people to know that the New Orleans sound came from him. But really, despite his strong feelings on this, even I, in my early years in music, knew that the New Orleans sound had been percolating and developing since the heyday of the infamous red light district Storyville and before. It comes from a shared New Orleans experience.

Once it started getting dark outside, I was finally invited into the house. He had a spinet piano in the living room and he started playing songs like, "Tipitina," "Ball the Wall," and "Junko Partner." It was a real treat to hear these classics. I couldn't believe that he was serenading me with his unique versions of these tunes. He'd just mention a song and, without missing a beat, set into playing it. It was entrancing to see and hear him comment on the music and play at the same time. As soon as he started playing the piano, the rest of the world melted away. Music even diverted him from his niece's antics.

I tried to record our conversation, but my cassette recorder was drowned out by the drone of the huge overhead fan. I just lived in the moment. I never thought I'd be fortunate enough to meet Professor Longhair, let alone be invited into his home and hear him play. Just as surprising was sharing a conversation and a drink for a couple of hours.

While in New Orleans, I was also trying to get in touch with Fats Domino, another great blues piano man. I called David Bartholomew, Fat's trumpet player and music director, who told me that Fats had left town to tour just the day before. When I mentioned that I'd wanted to interview Fats, Bartholomew invited me to his home for dinner. Bartholomew's wife and three daughters made me feel like a long lost relative. Afterward I heard him play with his band. I still have the photos to prove it.

Today, encounters like this seldom happen. Record companies and musicians demand control of their image. But in the 1960s, to be invited into musicians' homes and share their music was possible. These are treasured musical memories for me.

David Bartholomew, Fats Domino's music director, serenading me in his home in New Orleans in 1968.

B.B. KING

I saw B.B. King in concert thirteen times—a baker's dozen of immortal performances. B.B. was the consummate showman. Take the time he was headlining Melody Fair's tent facility with its revolving stage. He played his usual world class original blues hits, which included a particularly poignant version of "Why I Sing the Blues" for his encore. He walked the apron of the stage, pausing occasionally to shake the hand of an audience member. As the crowd's screams cross-faded with the final chord, BB pulled his gold-plated pocket watch out of his vest pocket and gave it to an extremely long-haired fan who had been particularly animated during the seventy-two minute set. I believe my jaw dropped.

B.B. was full of surprises. As he passed me backstage, he covered his mouth excusing himself, murmuring "I had onions for supper." Always the thoughtful gentleman. Since I'd seen him many times before, he remembered me and greeted me with a warm "Hello, young man. How are you?" I'm sure he didn't remember my name but he did remember me.

As I interviewed him in his dressing room, I mentioned how generous he was with his fans, impetuously giving away his time piece. He winked, put his forefinger across his lips and opened the lid of a brown shoe box near his guitar "Lucille." It was filled with pocket watches.

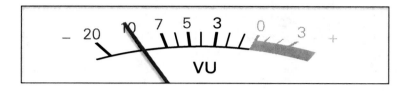

TEN

Walking off the Air

My defining moment in radio came on April 24, 1972. That was the day I walked off the air at WPHD-FM. It was my birthday, and you might say that I was mad as hell and I wasn't going to take it anymore. I remember waking up that morning, listening to the radio station, and suddenly realizing that the station didn't sound like my station anymore. The music was different. I called the DJ on the air to ask what happened. He told me that management had come in and reduced the library. The McLendon Corporation, Dallas-based owners of Buffalo's first freeform radio station, made the brilliant decision to cut the music library from 5,000 records to 500 and to put a lid on DJ chatter, especially political and social remarks. My rational response? I walked off the air in protest.

I probably should have read the writing on the wall about the McLendon Corporation in 1969 when I first met Jerry Garcia. Garcia and bassist Phil Lesh had come to Buffalo to play with the Buffalo Philharmonic Orchestra under the direction of Lukas Foss. I was told to do an interview, so I had my little tape recorder and I walked up to him and said, "Jerry, I made arrangements to interview you."

He said, "Okay."

"Is there any subject you'd like to avoid? Something you don't want to talk about?" I felt I was being thoughtful.

He responded sarcastically, "Well, it's your interview, man! What radio station do you work for?"

"WYSL-FM. It's owned by the McLendon Corporation."

The man, the hat, and the peace buckle in April 1972.

I thought Jerry would be impressed. After all, Gordon McLendon was a pioneer in the development of Top 40 programming, as well as "all news" radio.

Garcia snatched the microphone from my sweat-soaked hand, passed it between his legs and broke wind. Before I could react, the lead guitarist for the Grateful Dead flung the instrument of his flatulent rage to the floor and stomped offstage dropping an "F" bomb at me and McLendon.

In retrospect, my reaction to the management's decree about the albums might have been naïve. I was idealistic enough to believe in the American Dream and to believe that one person could make a difference. What I had come to accept as my right and duty—to play and say whatever I felt was appropriate on the air—was being compromised. I felt my only option was to walk away from the Big Brother that was trying to reel me in. I decided to leave a radio job that I loved, with a passion usually reserved for God and country to make a point and to maybe, just maybe, make a difference.

Throughout the day I'd made a bold decision, and I spoke to friends and colleagues to make sure they heard the show that night. As I drove to the station, I rehearsed the opening.

That night, I began my show with my statement: "Management has the right to do what they want because it is their station, but I also have the right to express myself." Tears welled in my eyes. I brought only one album with me to the station. I played the only song of my abbreviated shift, "Lather," by Jefferson Airplane, and walked off the air while the record played.

Lather was thirty years old today
They took away all of his toys.
His mother sent newspaper clippings to him
About his old friends who'd stopped being boys.
There was Harwitz E. Green, just turned thirty-three,
His leather chair waits at the bank.
And Sgt. Dow Jones, twenty-seven years old
Commanding his very own tank.

("Lather" – Jefferson Airplane)

Grace Slick wrote "Lather" as a biting indictment of the government's failure in Vietnam, as well as the assassinations of John and Bobby Kennedy and Martin Luther King Jr. echoed in Dion's *Abraham, Martin, and John.*

Dale Anderson, rock critic for the *Buffalo Evening News* at that time, described the event as follows:

FREEFORM ROCK RADIO IS TIED BY NEW RULES

This new (restrictive) format was adopted at Buffalo's progressive WPHD-FM on Monday, April 24, prompting one announcer to quit on the air. Three others are planning to leave.

Here's how it happened.

Jeff Lubick's last record faded and in came the deep archetypal FM radio voice of Jim Santella. A little tentatively because it wasn't just any Monday night. It was his 33rd birthday and his farewell to WPHD.

When he got through the "There comes a time ..." and told how he didn't begrudge owners the right to run their station and about certain conditions he couldn't work under, he played one last tune.

It was Jefferson's Airplane's "Lather" ... It summed up the moment for Jim and for WPHD and for what's happening in progressive rock radio across the nation.

Lubick held the station until program director Jack Robinson got there.

Meanwhile, Santella, WPHD's senior deejay, keeper of the prime-time 9 p.m. show, the man who introduced Buffalo to James Taylor, Chuck Mangione, and even Don McLean—Santella was gone ...

"He was too much into the music," Larry Levite (station manager) was saying a few days later. "It was a personal thing. The show was for him, not the audience. We're going to miss him but I think it was silly what he did on the air."

WPHD's format now requires deejays to play seventy-five percent of the music from a file of fifty top progressive albums, with the rest divided between new releases and oldies. Deejays were ordered to keep talking to the barest minimum. That's what provoked Santella.

"It would be different if Santella was the top deejay in the country," Larry notes. "Johnny Carson might have the right to quit on the air, but Jim ..."

There'd been a big photo of Santella in UB's student newspaper and a dedication naming him the "Man of the Year" for refusing to go along with "the totalitarian wave of the future in American media." Now strangers were greeting him in Norton Union. He hadn't wanted to make a big thing of it. Everything had been said.

"I never claimed to be that important," he said between sips of coffee, "but I don't like someone to push a button and I come out. I like relating to people as people."

WPHD had tightened up even before the format. Mandatory things kept burgeoning—more announcements, more commercials, more emphasis on just the top albums. Jim explained the restrictions.

"Once you start a flow, to me it stops when you have to do an ID or commercial. It DOES interrupt the flow of the program. It DOES put you in a format. Why push people into being automatons? Part of the overwhelming ennui today is because there are so few decisions you can make. Roles at one time were clearly defined and then Eli Whitney messed up the whole society with interchangeable parts.

"I'm not an interchangeable part. I want people to challenge me, make me find out where I'm at, and I should do that with other people too. You have to live what you are and what you think.

"I have no regrets. I think the audience has lost something. Not me, but something they could relate to."

(Dale Anderson, *Buffalo Evening News*, May 20, 1972)

In contrast to Larry Levite's opinion, Billy Altman, who went on to gain fame as a writer for *Creem* and *Rolling Stone* and was curator for the Rock and Roll Hall of Fame, wrote this:

"You gotta walk it like you talk it, or you lose that beat."

For courage above and beyond the call of countercultural duty, for Lou Reed integrity in the face of direct degradation, for steadfastly maintaining his gentility and equanimity in the face of the commercial onslaught of the cultural charlatans, the Institute for Rock 'n' Roll Studies presents the "First Annual Prodigal Sun Man of the Year Award" to Gentleman Jim Santella.

... Long dismayed by the continual erosion of artistic freedom and mounting cultural repression, Jim was faced Monday night with the prospect of the ultimate in restrictive and oppressive formats ... Confronted with this hypocrisy, one which is fast becoming the totalitarian wave of the future in American media, Jim refused to compromise his artistic and personal integrity.

This act of courage in the face of impending financial and professional ruin, cannot pass unacclaimed. We hope you will join with us in honoring Gentleman Jim Santella.

(Billy Altman, *UB Spectrum*, April 28, 1972)

THE INSTITUTE OF ROCK & ROLL

After walking off the air, I drove directly to UB's Fillmore Room where a Rock 'n' Roll Dance Party sponsored by the Institute of Rock & Roll was taking place. It was the kick-off event for a week-long celebration dedicated to popular music. I stopped on the way to purchase a half gallon bottle of wine. I spent the night dancing and drinking. It was quite a night.

I didn't have time to react to my decision to pull the plug on my radio career. I spent the next week helping the institute host a series of workshops and seminars. The institute was founded by a dozen or so rock enthusiasts to celebrate the keen interest in rock music as a historical, musical, and cultural phenomenon. I thought of them as my rock 'n' roll fraternity brothers. We were probably more like the nerds on *The Big*

Me and my Institute of Rock 'n' Roll Studies brothers, Eric Isralow, Ritchie Pacter, Billy Altman, Joe Fernbacher, Jeff Nesin, Gary Sperraza, and others. Dale Anderson missed picture day.

PHOTO BY ROBERT E. STODDARD, *BUFFALO EVENING NEWS*

Bang Theory. The event was sponsored by the S.A. (Student Association) and the G.S.A. (Graduate Student Association) Speakers Bureau.

Our group was led by Billy Altman, music editor of *The Spectrum*, and Jeff Nesin, destined to head up a pop culture curriculum at New York's School of Visual Arts. Other contributors included Joe Fernbacher, who used a stream-of-consciousness style to review albums without mentioning details; Gary Sperrazza, who was our seventeen-year-old writing wunderkind; Dale Anderson, music reviewer for *The Buffalo News*; and Richie Pachter, who would take his charming personality and knowledge of rock to a career at Warner Brothers' promotion department. I dipped my oar in the water, too, talking about the role of radio and rock 'n' roll. And, last but not least was the professor, Eric Isralow, who had an encyclopedic knowledge of rock 'n' roll. Unfortunately, the sands of time have erased my memory of other members.

The titles of some of the workshops we held hinted at the serio-comic nature of "new journalism." Eric gave two workshops: "The True Unadulterated History of Rock & Roll from 1950 to 1960" and "The Roots of Rock & Roll from 1960 to 1972."

I hosted a panel discussion on rock radio with legendary rhythm and blues DJ George "Hound Dog" Lorenz of WBLK-FM. The Hound was one of the early supporters of R & B. The first time I saw the Buffalo native at Kleinhans, he was hosting a touring caravan headlined by Etta James, Lloyd Price, and Little Willie John. I was surprised to find that the Hound was a slight, goateed man who walked with a limp. He was the only white man on the stage that night. As a teenager, I listened to him broadcasting from the Blue Room, his imaginary radio home. It was cool when he called Buffalo "Hound Town" and his fans "movers and groovers." I was awed to be in his presence.

Billy Altman was fond of saying, "There are only two kinds of music: good music and important music." I adopted his philosophy. Billy's workshop discussed the literary aspects of rock 'n' roll writing, enhanced by Jeff Nesin's and Dale Anderson's incisive comments and observations. They brought a whole lot of meat to the table. The thing that impressed me most was that each of them was knowledgeable about all aspects of the music. The workshops were never limited by their titles and most of them continued way past the scheduled time.

Later that year, the Rock & Roll Institute was instrumental in bringing Lou Reed to town. Arriving early in the day, he suggested we play a little one-on-one B-ball on one of the dormitory basketball courts near his motel. Billy, Jeff, Lou, and I played for less than an hour. Despite his being a big fan of the NY Knicks, let me just say that Lou Reed was no Earl the Pearl.

It was a heady week for all involved and full of fun. It certainly distracted me from the career-defining action of walking off the air. The word on the street was that I would never work in Buffalo radio again, but by now you know what that means. A month later, I was back on the air at WBFO-FM with an uber-underground rock show.

But life was not all champagne and roses.

A week after I walked off the air, Jeff Kaye, program director for Buffalo's WKBW, one of the most powerful AM stations in the country, pulled alongside my MGB at Delaware and Forest Avenue and called me a jerk for walking off the air. I flipped him the bird and proceeded to WBFO-FM, to do my shift. But I was really hurt. The big time, big voice, multitalented program director for Capitol Cities' flagship station had long been a role model for me. His re-creation of Orson Welles' 1938 Mercury Theater broadcast of *The War of the Worlds* in 1968 was monumental. It's another favorite radio memory of mine.

At this point, I began to doubt myself. Could it be I'd made a bad decision? It seemed that I was destined to be just a footnote in the history of Buffalo radio.

Looking back on it now, would I have made the same decision? Probably. It was a moment that has gone down in Buffalo's radio history.

The Thin, White Duke ... Bowie

Like Mick Jagger, David Bowie inhabits the androgynous world of rock, fame, fashion, and art. But, unlike the singular image of the Rolling Stones' messianic lead singer, Bowie created multiple exotic worlds populated with alter egos like Ziggy Stardust, Major Tom, and The Thin White Duke.

I shared a bottle of cognac and forty-five minutes of one-on-one conversation with David Bowie in his Hotel Statler suite on March 20, 1976. He had just finished a spectacular concert at the old Memorial Auditorium.

Even though he was running a fever that night, he still commanded the stage with an easy grace that carried over to our chat. He was charming and intelligent with a subtle sense of humor that was self-effacing but razor sharp. It was his playful wit and my openness that earned me the opportunity to meet him in person.

It all began with a telephone interview earlier in the day. But let me start from the *very* beginning. I was working middays at Q-FM 97, which put me in position to field a telephone interview that suddenly presented itself. I had just finished my shift when production director Steve Mitchell waved me into his studio, threw a set of headphones at me, and patched the phone into the Ampex 300. John McGhan, our program director, was supposed to do the interview, but he was out of the building. Mitchell called an audible and I got the ball. I introduced myself to a satiny smooth British voice and tried to act nonchalant.

It was Bowie.

My first question was designed to get him to say something complementary about our fair city: "How did you find Buffalo"?

He quipped without missing a beat, "We took a sharp left at Greenland" echoing the famous Beatles' retort when they first toured the states.

It was at that point that I lost my composure and blurted out, "You're nothing like your image." The statement must have tickled his fancy because he giggled, "And what would that be?"

I stuttered and replied weakly, "You know, more serious."

He replied in mock solemnity, "You mean stuffy."

Mitchell was twirling knobs and trying not to burst out laughing. The staff, which had gathered outside the studio when they found out that David Bowie was being interviewed, clutched their throats in the universal symbol of "you're choking!" I was thinking that I was about to blow the interview completely.

It didn't happen. I stopped trying to interview him and started just talking with him. I asked him about his stage outfits, especially those for Ziggy Stardust and Major Tom. He explained how he and his wife, Angela, designed all of his costumes. We also chatted about theater and film, especially Berthold Brecht and German Expressionism—my time in the UB theater department paid off. Bowie was apparently entertained by my straightforwardness and perhaps by my knowledge of his music and art school background. He invited me to meet him in person backstage.

I was psyched! Backstage with David Bowie! What could be cooler?

I went home, washed and polished my red MGB, and picked up my date, Janine, who was even more excited than I was. I was infatuated with Janine, a twenty-year-old math major at UB. She had a dimpled smile, a great sense of humor and could do a spot-on imitation of Grover from *Sesame Street*. When I bought a puppet of the irascible creature for Janine's birthday, she quickly learned how to make him come alive, much to my delight. She turned me on to the first two Genesis albums, and I reciprocated by introducing her to David Bowie, both metaphorically and actually. We had dinner, chatted like two magpies about what The Thin White Duke would wear and still arrived at Memorial Auditorium a full two hours early.

Powerful bright beams of light from the Super Troopers engulfed Bowie, dressed in a crisp white starched shirt and jet black pants, as he made his entrance. He glowed in the back lighting. The only thing better than his set-list, chosen from classics and new material, was the anticipation of actually meeting this rock god.

The concert ended, the obligatory encores were delivered, and we headed toward the backstage area where one of the security men delivered a crushing blow. "Bowie went straight to his limo. He wasn't feeling well." It looked like the meeting was not going to take place so we headed for the parking lot.

We hadn't taken two steps when a tall brunette with long hair asked, "Are you Jim Santella from Q-FM 97?" Her British accent disabused me of the notion that she was a local. "David has a fever but he said that you are welcome to join us at a small birthday party for one of the crew. He sent me to find you."

```
MGMBUFA BUF
2-020324E080002 03/20/76
ICS IPMMTZZ CSP
 1 7168375528 MGM TDMT BUFFALO NY 03-20 0208P EST


     western union  Mailgram

   JIM SANTELLA
   216 LASALLE
   BUFFALO NY 14214


   THIS MAILGRAM IS A CONFIRMATION COPY OF THE FOLLOWING MESSAGE:

    7168375528 TDMT BUFFALO NY 36 03-20 0208P EST
   PMS DAVID BOWIE, DLR
   ROCHESTER WAR MEMORIAL AUDITORIUM
   ROCHESTER NY



   800,000 UNITS OF PENICILLIN IS A REAL PAIN IN THE BOTTOM I HOPE YOU
   AND BARBARA AND COCOA ARE FEELING BETTER THANK YOU THANK YOU THANK
   YOU VERY MUCH FOR LAST NIGHT GOOD LUCK TONIGHT
    JIM SANTELLA AND JANINE

   1409 EST

   MGMBUFA BUF
```

800,000 units sounds like a lot, but it's really equivalent to about 500 mg. How did I know that?

I couldn't believe it! Despite a concert, a fever, and an intimate celebration, he remembered his invitation. Damn, I was impressed!

As Janine and I got off the Hotel Statler elevator and walked to one of the upper floor suites, I suddenly felt a huge calm wash over me. I was going to meet David Bowie and I was feeling as though the whole day had been a scene from a dream.

The door opened, Bowie extended his hand in greeting and led me to a coffee table in front of a couch. The first thing I noticed was the huge bottle of cognac and two delicate stemware glasses, which he filled halfway. Noticing Janine, he quickly asked for another glass. The second thing I noticed was that he had one brown eye and one green eye. For the next three-quarters of an hour, we sipped the smooth liquor slowly like two gentlemen in a Jane Austin novel. I must admit I completely forgot about Janine, who was sitting right next to me, as captivated by Bowie as I was.

I congratulated him on the success of *The Man Who Fell to Earth*, a film by Nicholas Roeg about an alien from a dying planet who comes to earth to try to replenish water supplies for his planet—the film had opened that night in New York City. We spoke about all things artistic: music, plays, films, his relationship with Mick Jagger, Studio 54, and the New York art and dance scene. I was taking courses in the Theatre Department and Media Studies and was able to easily talk the talk and walk the walk. My only real problem was trying not to stare at the reclusive rocker's mismatched eyes.

Oh yes, I did have one other slight problem: the cognac was so smooth I didn't even realize I was drunk. My speech wasn't slurred, I didn't stumble, and I wasn't sick to my stomach, but I was smart enough to know I needed to be driven home. Reluctantly, I handed Janine the keys to my MGB—she was the only other person I ever let drive my car. I awoke the next day with a clear head and I remembered that Bowie told me he was able to perform thanks to a shot of penicillin. I sent him a thank you telegram with a P.S.: "800,000 units of penicillin is a real pain in the bottom."

The next day, The Thin White Duke, who was twenty-nine at the time, was arrested along with Iggy Pop on a felony pot possession charge in Rochester. His mug shot looked regal and elegant. I don't think he ever took a bad picture. The camera definitely loved him.

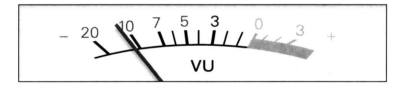

ELEVEN

Joel B. Williams

MOTHERS DON'T LET YOUR BABIES GROW UP TO BE COWBOYS

A little known secret of mine is my fascination with cowboys. I was an eight-year-old urban cowboy, forty-two years before John Travolta two-stepped his way across the silver screen.

It all started with a quarter. My mother would give me twenty-five cents, the price of admission at the Columbia Theater on Genesee Street. There, I followed the weekly adventures of singing cowboys like Gene Autry and Roy Rogers, masked cowboys like the Lone Ranger and Zorro, and whipsters like Lash LaRue and Whip Wilson.

Hopalong Cassidy and the Cisco Kid had comic sidekicks like Windy and Pancho. There were exotic range riders like the White Eagle and the Silver Avenger. Usually they were too dude for me. I wore twin six-shooters, slung low like my western heroes. My outfit was topped off by my dad's beat-up old fedora shaped into a cowboy hat. If I stayed more than fifteen extra minutes to catch the beginning of the second showing, I'd find myself yanked out of my gum-coated seat by my kid-wrangling mother. Otherwise, on the way home, I would usually chase imaginary rustlers, claim jumpers, and horse thieves up and down the Texas panhandle. Little did I suspect that one day I would get to be a cowboy at country station WWOL-FM—minus the pistols.

Now, what do my childhood fantasies about cowboys have to do with progressive radio, rock music, or Woodstock? I have no idea, except that I believe in serendipity, destiny, and enlightenment. To paraphrase Aldous Huxley, there are things known and things unknown, and in between are the doors of perception. Enough of this "cosmic debris." Let's return to the facts.

Although I was known for wearing a black cowboy hat and boots, I have been on a horse exactly one time in my life, and the ride lasted less than thirty seconds. It was the summer of 1971, I was working at WPHD-FM, and Jack Robinson, my program director from Dallas, Texas, said he wanted to go out riding. I guess he thought that since Buffalo was in *western* New York, horse stables would be plentiful.

Jeff Lubeck, our evening jock, owned a few horses, and he took Jack and me out to where he boarded them. He gave me a quick lesson that emphasized pulling on the reins of my horse to show him "who's boss." That's when I began to have second thoughts about climbing onto a 900 pound animal that was all muscle. A horse is not like a dog that you walk up to and pet. It's a big animal that doesn't really like you yanking on his mouth.

Well, we got on our horses, started cantering toward the trails, and before I knew it, there goes my program director, riding across the horizon like a pony express rider delivering the mail. It was a short ride. He flew over his horse's head and landed in six inches of mud. That was enough for me. I got off my horse immediately. If the kid from the Lone Star state couldn't stay in the saddle, what chance did I have? I've not mounted a horse since, but I did borrow the cowboy image and came to be known as "Joel B. Williams, the Midnight Cowboy" after I found myself banned from rock radio for walking off the air.

WWOL-FM

Let me tell you a little about my year as a cosmic cowboy at WWOL-FM. I loved both the job and the music.

One day, my good friend Al Wallack called to say that WWOL, a country/western station, was looking for an overnight DJ. My response to the offer was that I didn't know anything about country/western music. What would I say? Al said, "You don't need to say anything. Just shut up and play the music." Still convinced that I would never get a job in radio after the debacle at WPHD, I went to see the program director,

Bobby Knight ("your 300-pound alarm clock"), who was from out of town and didn't really know anything about me. He liked my air check and thought I could do the job, but he told me that he wanted me to change my name. There was already someone working at the station whose name was Jim Sotet, and Bobby was afraid there would be too much confusion with our last names sounding so much alike. So he said, "Change your name."

I said, "Okay, what do I change it to?"

Bobby asked, "Do you have a middle name?"

I said, "Yes, William." And then I suddenly thought of my college roommate, Joel DiBartolo. I had always liked his name, so I said, "Joel Williams. Joel Williams, yes that's it!"

I went home and I wrote out some ID cards using my new name: Joel Williams, Joel Williams. Somehow it still didn't sound quite right. At the time I was listening to a lot of California disc jockeys, but there was one New York DJ whose name rang a bell: B. Mitchell Reed. I loved that arrangement. B. Mitchell Reed. There was a lot of character to a middle name. Hence, Joel B. Williams was born. "Hello, this is Joel B. Williams on WWOL." Okay, I'm ready.

My goal for many years was to be an expert in the history of all popular American music of the twentieth century, an ambitious goal and much too difficult to achieve. Yet, that was what drove my overreaching musical hubris. Working at WWOL gave me insight into the role of three American musical tributaries: blues, jazz, and country. But it wasn't always that way. I was smart enough to know what I didn't know and followed Al's advice. I didn't say anything about the music, just: "That was Porter Waggoner; coming up next is Loretta Lynn with "Coal Miner's Daughter.""

One night, I found a song that I thought I knew something about; I played "Act Naturally." As it ended, I turned on the microphone and back-announced the song: "That was Buck Owens doing the old Beatles' tune, "Act Naturally." This is WWOL, Joel B. Williams, your Midnight Cowboy ..." and before I could finish the backsell, the phone bank lit up. I thought, wow, everyone loves Beatles music.

I picked up the phone. "You idiot! Buck Owens wrote "Act Naturally," not the Beatles. Get your facts straight, Joel B.!" I learned an important lesson: Always check your facts and don't underestimate your audience, especially if they are country music fans.

THE SOUND OF AMERICA

1120 AM-104.1 FM

WWOL

SCOTT CASSIDY
WWOL 6 · 10

DAVID R. SNOW
WWOL 10 · 3

BOBBY KNIGHT
WWOL 3 · 7

NICK SENECA
WWOL 7 · 12

JOEL B. WILLIAMS
WWOL 12-6

My first appearance in front of a packed house of country music fans drew a thundering roar of silence at Kleinhans Music Hall. That's right. Joel B.'s faithful overnight listeners sat on their hands as I made my appearance from the wings. Before the concert started, Bobby Knight (remember him, the 300-pound morning alarm clock?) welcomed the audience, stroked the headliner, who that evening was Sonny James, and then introduced the on-air staff. Nick Seneca, our evening guy, was bright as a silver dollar in his crisp blue jeans, matching shirt, and tie. He waved his chocolate-brown cowboy hat at the crowd and drew high-pitched squeals of delight from female fans.

David R. Snow, the epitome of country authenticity, was our afternoon drive-time jock. All he had to do was say his name and the station call letters and you knew he was the real deal. He wore a form-fitting cowboy shirt with stitching around the pockets. He bowed, said, "Howdy," and the crowd whistled and stomped, making the balcony shake with their rip-roaring greeting.

Our morning jock, Scott Cassidy, wore a straw hat, baggy pants, and looked like he had just finished plowing the south forty and didn't have time to comb his unruly straw-colored hair.

I planned an auspicious entrance. I wore my black cowboy hat, black cowboy boots, black coattails, and black bib overalls. I was channeling the "man in black" himself, Johnny Cash. My hair and beard were black and hippy-long. Not only was I dressed to kill, I planned to make *my* entrance from the opposite side of the stage, carrying a broom and sweeping my way downstage. I thought I'd get a laugh. Bobby announced, "Would you put your hands together and welcome the newest member of the WWOL family, Joel B. Williams,

Joel B. Williams on stage at the Erie County Fair in 1973.

your Midnight Cowboy!" With that he gestured to the right. Nick, David, and Scott turned to the right. I made my entrance from the left sweeping the stage like a wayward janitor. Bobby didn't notice me and directed me not to be shy. "Come meet your fans, Joel B." The silence knocked the wind out of my sails. It was at that moment that I fully understood the pictures that radio created in the minds of listeners. I had not measured up to what my voice promised. It wasn't the first time I had been told "You don't look like your voice!" Like many DJs, I believe I had a face made for radio.

Later that night, I learned another lesson: country artists, at least in the 1970s, were polite, self-effacing, and down to earth. Sonny James, the headliner, came over to me from his dressing room and introduced himself. "Hi, Joel B., would you mind if I had my picture taken with you?" I couldn't believe it. Sonny James, who had twenty-three charted singles and a monster number one hit with "Young Love" was asking for permission to have his picture taken with me! He took the time and effort to introduce himself and make me feel important. Then he gave me an autographed 8x10 glossy photograph of him. I still have it in my scrapbook: "Joel B., my best to you, Sonny."

The lesson from Sonny James was clear to me. No matter how big you get, don't let a swelled head get in the way of being kind. I loved working at WWOL, discovering legendary country outlaw singers like Hank Williams, Johnny Cash, George Jones, Merle Haggard, Waylon Jennings, and Willie Nelson. I had a passion for Waylon Jennings's "Mammas Don't Let Your Babies Grow Up to Be Cowboys."

Of course, there were always advantages to my radio audience not being able to see me. There is absolutely no correlation between what a jock's voice sounds like and what he looks like. Take me, for instance. On the air I look like a combination of Paul Newman, Robert Redford, and George Clooney. In person, I more closely resemble Curley, Larry, and Moe. In contrast, John Farrell had a voice that the gods envied but barely weighed 135 pounds.

Most importantly, though, working alone overnight in a dark studio gave me the opportunity to do things I would never have the nerve to try otherwise. Like the night at WWOL when I got the bright idea to challenge my audience to a game of strip hangman. One minute I was talking about playing Whack-A-Mole at the Erie County Fair, and the next, Joel B. was talking about a new twist to playing hangman.

Noncontact games aren't any fun. For instance, hangman isn't challenging unless it's high stakes hangman like Vegas poker tournaments. So, to spice up the game, I added a wild card to the seven-step word game. Each caller represented the entire audience. For every wrong answer, everyone removes an article of clothing. If you are right, I remove something. If the audience wins the game, I read the 3 a.m. news in the nude. I trusted my listeners to be honest.

I knew I could control the game, because I would choose the questions. I'd let the audience win the first two rounds and then throw a no-hitter for the rest of the game. It sounded like fun. The first two rounds went well. I threw one boot and then another against the studio wall. Both callers were women and flirtatious. In fact, all of the callers were women, flirtatious *and* correct. I lost my shirt, pants, and t-shirt. My socks were the only thing that stood between me and modesty. I lost them, too. Once again, I underestimated my audience. Reading the 3 a.m. news that night, I had to turn down the air conditioning.

TWELVE

Out of the Country and Back to the City

THE MICK AND THE ROOSTER

At this time, I had three sources of income: WWOL, Lockwood Library, and landlord. Combined, they gave me financial independence. I had purchased a two-family home on LaSalle Avenue in the University District and the rent from the upstairs apartment paid my mortgage. My second front, CSEA library job, paid the rest of my expenses. This was important to me because it allowed me to make radio career decisions based on artistic merit rather than financial necessity. It was difficult to get fired from a state job and as a supervisor I could take off any time I needed.

For example, in August 1974, my good friend Andy Fisher and I were walking out of the UB library after work talking about my favorite baseball player ever, Mickey Mantle, who was being inducted into the Baseball Hall of Fame the next day. You could practically see the light bulbs go off over our heads. We looked at each other in the parking lot and Andy said, "Wouldn't it be neat to see The Mick inducted?"

I said, "I can take the day off. Let's do it." The next day we woke up bright and early and were on the road to the Cooperstown museum.

The New York Yankee slugger was in rare form. He was more than tipsy; he was sloshed. The result was some intimate dugout stories, like the time when he, southpaw pitcher Whitey Ford, and second baseman Billy Martin, came in after curfew only to find manager Casey Stengel holding court with sports reporters in the hotel lobby, blocking their entrance. Their solution was for one of them to climb over the transom and open the side entrance. Skinny Billy Martin was chosen for the task. Ford and Mantle boosted him up and over. He disappeared into the hotel, leaving his teammates stranded. They ended up sleeping in the alley.

He also told a story about how lucky he was to have good financial advisors. All he needed was to contribute his name. "Mr. Youngman built a Holiday Inn in Joplin, Missouri, and called it Mickey Mantle's Holiday Inn. And we were doin' pretty good there, and Mr. Youngman said, 'You know, you're half of this thing, so why don't you do something for it.' So we had real good chicken there and I made up a slogan … I said, 'To get a better piece of chicken, you'd have to be a rooster.' And I don't know if that's what closed up our Holiday Inn or not, but we didn't do too good after that." The country boy was never noted for his subtlety.

BACK TO RADIO

I always thought that successful DJs shared three unassailable qualities: a monster ego that even Howard Stern couldn't top, a wicked sense of humor that could give a concussion to a blitzing linebacker, and a hide as thick as a Serengeti bull elephant. As for me, three Sky Masterson traits, luck, luck, and luck, were my guardian angels. And 1974 would prove to be quite a transitional year for me—once again, luck brought me back to WPHD.

I had to leave WWOL in the spring of 1974 due to illness. Burning the candle at both ends led to a bout of pneumonia. I was off the air for a while, but I continued my library job. Then I got a phone call from John McGhan at WPHD. McGhan was the sweetest, smoothest program director I have ever worked for. He could coax the gold fillings out of your teeth he was so persuasive. David Cahn, who was working in Buffalo radio at this time and later became a promotion man for Warner Brothers records, convinced McGhan that what they needed for the station was me. John convinced general manager Larry Levite, whom I had walked out on in 1972, to rehire me. McGhan also talked me into offering up the requisite *mea culpa* to Levite.

WPHD – A STATION RISES FROM ASHES

Yeah! I was back at WPHD. The prodigal son had returned. I was working with a staff of experienced FM rockers who knew what they were doing. I had worked with all of them before and they were great. We might not have had the total freedom that I usually enjoyed, but it was still better than any job that would've pleased my mom. And I was back to three incomes. With minimum interference from management, we did what needed to be done to increase the ratings. Remember, in 1969 the FM radio audience was very small. By 1974, FM radio was overtaking AM radio to become the dominant platform for popular music. One of the reasons, besides the music, was that automobile manufacturers had started installing FM radios as standard equipment. The station went so far as to offer FM conversion kits as prizes for those with AM-only radios in their car.

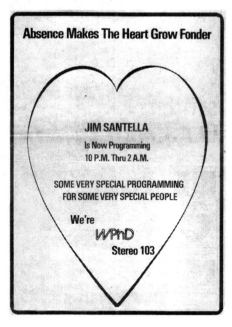

An ad-worthy comeback. In the *Buffalo New Times* on April 7, 1974.

> "We were in the process of evolving from being a freeform station into a well-oiled machine ready to assault the AM monster," [said David Cahn.] McGhan was the perfect guy to lead that assault. He was driven: radio was his life, and he was on a mission. He brought a sense of professionalism to the station, but he was also an outrageous showman.
>
> "McGhan was like a cheerleader, but he was a true believer," Santella says. "He was not a great jock or a music maven, but he was a manager in the best sense of the word. He totally loved radio."
>
> (Anthony Violanti, *The Buffalo News*, October 14, 1990)

Quadrophonic 103

Promotion was McGhan's strong suit. He was our P. T. Barnum. Later on, John made a big name for himself in Pittsburgh radio and went on to produce radio and TV nationally. He worked for Rolling Stone Productions and co created and co produced *NBC Friday Night Videos*, a precursor of MTV. He also helped launch Ted Turner's Cable Music Channel, which became VH1.

WPHD-FM was actually more commercial than it had ever been, but it worked. A perfect balance of art and commerce, it was the key to the future. It would turn out to be the Top 40 of the '70s.

Buffalo Evening News music critic, Dale Anderson, may have put it best when he wrote about the station:

[WPHD's new programming] is still tied to the ratings game, of course. The old progressive philosophies, which tended to be of the this-is-our-music variety, are roundly condemned now as "serving an elitist segment of the audience."

The new theories are kind of a populist version of the old ones. It's everybody's music now. In fact it's everybody's everything. "Special programming for special people" is the catch phrase. (John) McGhan likens the whole thing to "what the general store was to a small town."

... The station seems stronger than ever. Not only in the ratings, which are up and promise to go higher but also in corporate support and the quality of the on-the-air work. Things are crisper now, better throughout. "It's part of the evolution of progressive radio," [David] Cahn explains. "We want to stop people from thinking it's an acid-rock jukebox, which it absolutely is not," McGhan says. "We're trying to compete, of course. We're offering such a variety.

"Steve Lapa, our music director, was at WCMF [in Rochester] too, and he's a strong afternoon man. He keeps telling Sandy Beach and J. J. Gordon to watch out 'cause he's gonna bury them."

Beyond Lapa, the line-up these days is Randy Hock, mornings, McGhan, middays, Cahn early evenings, Hank Ball at night and Ron Reeger ... pinch-hitting on the weekends.

Ironically, the symbolic hero at the old WPHD returned to the studios this week to do the late evening show, two years after he quit on the air in one of the station's first philosophical upheavals.

It's Gentleman Jim Santella, he of the beard, the cowboy hat, and the low, low voice. But elitists shouldn't get their hopes up. Santella's done time on the graveyard shift at a country music station. Seems he's become a progressive populist too.

(Dale Anderson, *Buffalo Evening News,* March 23, 1974)

It may have been a populist station, but the audience loved it and we were able to take chances with the music. Once on my show, I spent thirty minutes going from one Frank Zappa cut to another. But our bubble was about to burst.

WPhD stereo 103.3
Buffalo, New York

LOYALIST I.D.

Name _____

Address _____

PhD Listener No. ___12180___

Bob Howard, from Washington, DC, bought WPHD and changed the letters back to WYSL-FM. Howard said he was not going to change the format, and I made the mistake of believing him. But, as we found out later, Howard was going to make the station a rock station without any progressive content. Larry Levite, station manager, was the first to see the writing on the wall and made the jump to WEBR and hired Steve Lapa as program director. Everyone at WPHD lost their job—me, McGhan, Tom Teuber, everyone.

My final shift at WPHD was a special one. Peter Wolf, vocalist for the J. Geils Band who had worked as a DJ on WBCN-FM in Boston prior to Charles Laquidara, did the show with me. Steve Lapa offered me a job at WEBR, an easy-listening station, and I took it. Hey, a job is a job! I wanted to be on the radio.

Q-FM 97 AND THE SUPERSTARS FORMAT—1975

Over at WEBR-AM I was playing Anne Murray, Andy Williams, Carole King, and more music that I thought I could stand. Wrong. By the time two weeks had passed, I knew I'd made a mistake. One night while on the air, the red studio "Batphone" rang. My guardian angel tapped me on the shoulder. It was the sweet-talking John McGhan who had resurfaced at WGRQ-FM.

> "He asked me [Jim Santella] if I wanted to come to work with him at WGRQ, which was doing poorly as a high energy rock station (instituted on New Year's Eve 1973) and was changing its format. He told me that under this new format there would be no room for experimentation at all."
>
> (Philip Bashe, *Foxtrot*, May 25, 1977)

The conversation went something like this:

McGhan: How would you like to work in real radio?

Santella: When do we start?

McGhan: The format is set. No choices.

Santella: OK. When do we start?

McGhan: You understand you have to follow the format.

Santella: Got it. When do we start?

No one could get me to follow a format, except the ever persuasive McGhan. He had a patented catchphrase: "We've got to be fabulous today!" That always brought out the best in us. He was the best cheerleader I ever knew and became a close friend. I miss him to this day.

Q-FM 97, now known as 97 Rock, was born. The station celebrated its fortieth anniversary in February 2015. It switched from a format called Super Q—a rocker format—to Album Oriented Radio (AOR). All the old gang from WPHD was back and on the air at Q-FM 97. It was to be my home for the next five years.

We spent a weekend converting to the new SuperStars format, created by radio consultant Lee Abrams. McGhan was right, there were no choices. There was a box of 3x5 cards that dictated the music that would be played—about 500 album titles and the song to be played from each album. It was like a Chinese menu: one from column A, two from Column B.

As I recall, there were seven categories, known simply as A, B1 and B2, C, and so on. The "A" category was the newest, hottest albums. "B1" was recent music, called recurrents, from the last six months. "B2" included music from the six months before that. There was a classic hits category ... You get the idea. The format was set and there was no getting around it. Wink, wink, nudge, nudge. But the good news was, there was more than one cut allowed from an album. Abrams' format would dominate popular radio for decades. It may not have been creative, but it worked. It got people listening in large numbers, replacing the Top 40 singles of the 1960s.

It was on February 10, 1975, that the Q went on the air as an AOR station. It's a tightly programmed station that uses Lee Abrams' new SuperStars format. As McGhan promised, there is little room for experimentation and at times this does make the station seem almost sterile. But the music is bright and familiar and it's easy to see why the Q (Q-FM 97) has a sizable audience. Its air personalities at times seem too homogenous, but they are all solid professionals, led by Santella himself, one of the most popular and respected disc jockeys in all of Western New York.

(Philip Bashe, *Foxtrot*, May 25, 1977)

I worked the night shift, 10 p.m. to 2 a.m. I especially loved these hours. The night time was the right time for me to segue through our music library. I discovered that few management people, if any, listened after midnight, so I took a few liberties in what I played. Maybe the cut I wanted was right next to the required song on the album. It wouldn't have been 180 degrees from the format, just music I thought fit in and should be played. Genesis' "Watcher of the Skies" would fall into that category. I figured the first song management caught me on would get me a warning. I never got that warning and garnered a lot of satisfaction from what I played, as did listeners.

The concerts at Rich Stadium began about this time too. I introduced a lot of bands there, and I still have the cowboy hats to prove it. Some of my favorites included Judy Collins, Seals and Crofts, Emerson, Lake and Palmer, Yes, The Eagles, Crosby, Stills, Nash, and Young, and Bob Seeger. They were really rowdy events. Prior to this, concerts were in bars and small venues. Arena rock was a new concept. Rock music was getting even bigger. It was a way to reach a lot more people and make a lot more money.

Promoters like Harvey and Corky, as well as Festival East Concerts made quite a living from booking arena rock concerts. Arenas were great for the bands, but it was a different audience experience. Instead of hearing your favorite band up close and personal, now the audience was a mass of people with really loud sound. It was a new kind of group experience. It was the event that was important. Concerts turned into huge parties for you and 70,000 of your closest friends. Needless to say, the audience loved it.

McGhan was still at Q-FM 97 in 1977, and he got it in his head that I should switch from evenings to midday. The only problem was that I was still working full-time at the UB library for $9,000 a year—the same amount I was making at Q-FM. At that time, $18,000 was a damned good salary. McGhan managed to convince me to give up the library job, work middays, and agreed to pay me $10,000. In other words, he got me to take an $8000 pay cut and change my shift. John was more than persuasive. He practically picked my pocket. What really convinced me was when he asked me, "Are you a librarian or are you a radio guy?" No one could say no to McGahn, and who was I to be the exception.

To this day my wife, Mary Lou Wiltberger, still chides me for my lack of business acumen, quitting my job at the library just weeks before I reached the ten-year mark, which would have guaranteed me some retirement income from New York State. Not only that, when the opportunity was available decades later to regain that money by working just one day for the state, I never did it. My wife loves me, but if she'd gotten me to work that one day, I'm sure she'd love me even more.

Soon after that, our morning man John Rivers went to Chicago. McGhan got that look in his eye and my shift changed again. I had more listeners than ever during that time. Working mornings was a whole new ballgame. I could not be my laid back self. I loved working nights.

I could feel the audience breathe. I was able to answer calls and still play the music. Mornings were a much faster pace. Songs were shorter. There were traffic, weather, and sports scores to announce, and I did crossovers with the news announcers. I'd arrive an hour early to write my ad libs and jokes and swig enough high-octane coffee to get my motor running. I adopted the Boy Scout motto: be prepared. Suddenly, there were all sorts of people around and I was part of the everyday activities of the station. It was a great time.

As the morning DJ, I did lots of promotions and contests. It was another way to connect with the audience. I always made sure they had fun. In 1977, Randy Newman's song "Short People" came out and it tickled my fancy, so I played it to no end. I played it so much, that I started the official "Short People's Club." Men had to be under 5'5" and women had to be 5' or shorter. Meetings for the club were held in bars, and you could get in for free if you had your little yellow membership card, signed by yours truly. On those nights the bars resembled Munchkinland. At 5'11" I was the only exception. The "Short People's Club" got me a cute new date, Fern, who was about 4'11". Ironically, she left me for a shorter guy.

I even enjoyed "S and M in the morning." Sound kinky? Not really. It stood for "Santella and Mary in the morning." It seems that all of the important women in my life have been named Mary, starting with my mom and including my wife, Mary Lou.

The next important Mary in my life was Mary van Vorst, the morning news lady. I discovered it was great to interact with someone else on the air. We even had special stationery printed with our program logo. Despite the title, unlike the usual sexual innuendo of other morning radio teams, we were like a bickering brother and sister. I would make a point of having some gem of information to tease Mary with daily. It might be something as simple as kidding her about the backward ways of her home state, Montana, or her bouncy red hair. Since our exchanges ended with the news, Mary would always have the last word:

> *Mary:* Jim.
>
> *Jim:* Yes, Mary.
>
> *Mary:* Turn off your microphone.

We worked together for only a short time but have remained close friends for life.

Out in the community supporting a good cause.

Mary and I also had a weekly three-way interview with Reggie McKenzie of the Buffalo Bills, one of the first radio teams to do this kind of show, I believe. McKenzie, who was one of the guards on the famous Electric Company offensive line, kept us informed as to what was going on with the team. He was not only informative, he also had a great sense of humor and was very entertaining.

On October 31, 1979, I opened with "Trick or Treat," and McKenzie treated us to one of our biggest scoops. There'd been a lot of speculation, but Reggie told us that it might be one of the last times that we'd see O. J. Simpson in a Bills uniform. It turned out, he was absolutely right.

Life was full. I was working six days a week, deejaying at Stage One a couple nights a week, or just going out to hear music. These were my party years. According to the 1977 poster that hangs on my studio/office wall, the "Official Results" of the "Q-FM Buffalo to Los Angeles Music Poll" voted me the *Best Buffalo DJ*. Imagine that. Partying had its rewards. Things were definitely going well for me.

Until 1980, that is. By this time, McGhan had left for WDVE-FM in Pittsburgh. His replacement, program director Johnny Velchoff, was leaving for Texas and I really wanted that job. I always felt I'd make a good program director. I thought I had the best chance because I had the most experience and had been there the longest. Four of us at the station were in contention: me, Bob MacRae, my lifelong friends Jim Pastrick and Pat Feldballe. Pastrick was a production engineer extraordinaire and Feldballe's ubiquitous voice can be heard on everything from Time-Life records to WGRZ-TV's local commercial voiceovers. I ruled out Pastrick and Feldballe, because as good as they were, they didn't have a long history with FM radio at that time and MacRae didn't seem to put much effort into his show. He began wearing a brand new suit and tie, though, and I thought he was schmoozing up to station manager Jim Difiglia to plead his case.

This time luck was not with me and, sure enough, MacRae was hired, despite the fact that none of us felt he was right for the job. The first we heard of it was not from management, but when MacRae was interviewing Charlie Daniels and he congratulated MacRae on his new position! But nothing was improving and our ratings were not going up. After two months, just before MacRae lost his job, he fired me, even though he didn't have the power to do that.

WACJ-FM, a '60s oldies station, was my next port of call. Program director Dan Cottone hired me. I really enjoyed playing that music and thought it would be successful. It lasted only two months, when the format changed to Good Times and Oldies, a '50s oldies format. I was beginning to feel like the DJ in Harry Chapin's *W-O-L-D*, moving from station to station. I then did a short stint at WZIR-FM, a progressive station on Grand Island. It was deja vu all over again. WZIR was looking for a new program director and I was up for the job. But can you believe it? Who do you think they hired? That's right: Bob MacRae. He said "Let's bury the hatchet." Then he proceeded to bury it right in my head and fired me once again. Shortly thereafter, he also lost his job.

Radio is a funny business.

Summerfest

As Sky Masterson sings in *Guys and Dolls*, "Luck Be a Lady Tonight." In my experience, radio and crap shooting both thrive on an abundance of luck. I got my first radio job by luck and lost it four months later by luck—bad luck, and four months later I was hired back by the same station that fired me. Luck, good and bad, has always been an important part of my success.

My mother, who lived through the Depression, never believed I had a real job, luck or no luck. She believed radio was populated by snake oil salesmen. Oh, it was fun to listen to entertainers like Burns and Allen, Jack Benny, *Lux Radio Theater* and *Suspense*, but it ranked with used car salesmen and ambulance chasers on the hierarchy of respectable occupations. My sister was a teacher, my brother managed Turgeon brothers' restaurants, and my cousin Bill was an accountant. That kind of work mom could understand. I tried to please her.

At Grover Cleveland High School, I learned to type (the most useful course I ever took), and I took two years of double-entry bookkeeping that I never used. But being a DJ wasn't a job for momma's first born. I readily agree. It's not the kind of work that demands rocket science mentality. There are not a lot of Mensa members working in radio. Can you imagine Albert Einstein as a DJ? "Good morning all you E=MC Squared cats. What's the difference between a DJ and a US savings bond? Eventually one of them matures."

Mom wanted me to graduate from college as a lawyer. She claimed I had the gift of gab. I claimed I was inoculated with a phonograph needle! Brevity may be the soul of wit but, as my good friend Jim Pastrick revealed at my induction into the Buffalo Broadcasters Hall of Fame in 2005, "Ask Santella for the time, he'll tell you how to build a clock." I'm not going to tell you how to build a clock, but I do intend to tell you about my interview with Sweet Judy Blue Eyes that found me at a loss for words.

The date was July 20, 1975; the location, a remote studio van backstage at Rich Stadium; the event, a Summerfest concert. The Eagles were headlining, and Seals and Crofts, Dan Fogelberg, and Judy Collins rounded out the huge outdoor event.

Bear with me here. I'm terrified of water—have I mentioned that? After years of denial, I now admit it. I suffer from aquaphobia. I've even started my own twelve-step program: "Hi, I'm Jim Santella and I'm an aquaphobe." Friends, relatives, and even some excellent lifeguards have all taken a shot at teaching me how to swim, to no avail.

I've taken tadpole swimming lessons and been embarrassed by two-year-olds who swam like Esther Williams. I enrolled in YMCA swimming lessons and the swim instructor got to calling me "Stoney," a reference to my inability to float even with a kickboard. It's not that I didn't try. I've gone as far as getting prescription water goggles. Now when I put my head underwater, I can see my fears more clearly.

But it was my interview with Judy Collins that would nearly push me into the deep end. Like Ulysses lured by the Sirens, I nearly succumbed to a pair of limpid pools of turquoise that threatened to drown me in their luminosity.

I was working at Q-FM 97, the precursor to 97 Rock. The staff consisted of morning man John Rivers, whose bright red beard made him look like Animal from *The Muppet Show*. Tom Teuber was our stoic music director and midday guy. He was as solid as the Rock of Gibraltar. Program director John McGhan held down the afternoon drive-time slot and honcho-ed the troops. I was the evening jock. Last but not least was Skip Edmunds who plied his love for Genesis, Nazareth, and Pink Floyd overnight and under the covers. It was an experienced crew of lean, mean, and dangerous-to-know FM veterans. We had honed our swords on the legendary WPHD-FM air waves.

Nine months earlier the entire staff had been fired from WPHD-FM when a transfer of ownership put us all in line at the New York State Unemployment Office. Now we were "Baaaaack!" All of us were experienced at covering remote broadcasts in arena and stadium-sized venues. Arena concerts drew in tens of thousands more fans than a club, and bands and promoters could not pass up that revenue. One large venue concert earned more money than five small venue gigs.

Preparation and redundancy were key elements of our coverage. Q-FM 97 roadies and stage techs arrived a full day early to set up instruments, amps, and mics. The night before the concert, our engineers drove the station van to Rich Stadium, connected telephone lines from the backstage area to the station and tested and retested all lines. Early the next morning, Rivers and I arrived at 6 a.m. with gallons of caffeine and dozens of sugar bombs ready to jump start us while we retested all lines.

Rivers, who was the booth announcer, handled all the transitions, IDs, and station format. He was smooth, spontaneous, and slick. I did the color and interviews. It wasn't unusual for me to have dozens of 5x7 cards filled with info-bits, one-liners, or prepared questions. The first time Rivers saw my mountain of cards, he blurted out, "What are those, your ad-libs?"

"No," I snapped back. "Too bad your mother didn't keep the stork and throw you out with the bath water." We really worked well together.

John McGhan, our charming cheerleader, did all the stage announcements, schmoozed the stage manager, and kept the energy level sky high. He had a way with the band members, concert crowds, and industry reps. "Good morning, Buffalo. I'm John McGhan, program director of Q-FM 97. Welcome to Summerfest '75. Are you ready to rock? How many of you are here for Judy Collins? Dan Fogelberg? Seals and Crofts? The Eagles? How many came to party all day and all through the night? Me too!"

McGhan had a way with the audience. They trusted him. On this particular day the huge crowd started lining up in the Rich Stadium parking lot, and, when the gates were opened, a flood of fans crowded down next to the stage, putting pressure on the structure. As more and more fans arrived they took up residence against the stage front and McGhan was enlisted to get the crowd to back up ten feet to relieve the pressure. He shifted into schmooze mode. "We are blessed with great weather today and 72,000 seats to fill, not counting the field. How many of you brought a blanket to sit on?" The crowd waved a rainbow of brightly colored cloth. "How many of you brought 'goodies'?" Again the crowd stood up, cheered, and waved everything from potato chips to hash pipes. McGhan had one more comment. It reminded me of Chip Monk at Woodstock. "We need to move our 'stuff' back ten feet. Reach out behind you and grab." Like a crowd of kindergartners following their

In the Q-FM 97 van, broadcasting a live interview with Peter Frampton during a Rich Stadium Summerfest concert in the mid-1970s.

teacher, everyone played grab-ass, moved their "stuff" and had fun without feeling restricted.

The first performer was Dan Fogelberg. His rich baritone voice turned a massive Rich Stadium concert into an intimate coffee house-like performance during his tight, thirty-minute set. Both artificial "grass" and the more natural-smelling weed provided a mild contact high for audience, performer, and stage hands alike. Seals and Crofts, with their acoustic-friendly set had the ladies in the audience swirling and dancing to gems like "Diamond Girl" and "Summer Breeze." The eighty-plus degree temperature and pot-drenched atmosphere turned the mellow dial up to high.

My interview with Seals and Crofts was as smooth as peanut butter. Sitting side-by-side in the interview van with halos of matching cherubic black curls, they looked like bright-eyed Buddhas finishing each other's sentences. To be perfectly honest, I don't remember one memorable thought they expressed. They did use the word "man" a lot. Flipping through my 5x7 cards, I conducted a three-minute, fast-paced interview that got me a smile from their road manager. The interview ended with Rivers thanking the duo and reminding our audience at home that Judy Collins would be our next guest. I had forty-five minutes to prepare for the next interview, or so I thought.

When Seals and Crofts exited the van, I glanced at my Judy Collins notes, turning my back to Rivers who was trying desperately to catch my attention. "Jim, you lucky dog," he said. "Ms. Collins asked if we could interview her now. She is going to get her wish. Ladies and gentlemen, Sweet Judy Blue Eyes—Judy Collins!" I turned around and there I was face-to-face with two of the largest, bluest eyes I had ever seen. I was speechless. Rivers rode to my rescue. "Welcome to Buffalo, Ms. Collins."

I added a weak, "You really do have blue eyes." Judy winced, I blushed and McGhan, who had escorted Judy to the van, was waving desperately at Rivers to do something. The silence was thunderous. Rivers put the mic to his mouth just as I started reading from my cue card. "Judy, thank you so much for being with us today." Then I launched into my best Bob Costas' everything-but-the-kitchen-sink question.

"You are the oldest of five siblings. You were born in Seattle, Washington, and moved to Denver, Colorado, when you were ten. You were extremely musical. In fact, you studied classical piano with Antonia Brico, making your public debut at age thirteen performing Mozart's Concerto for Two Pianos. Your teacher held high hopes for your classical piano career. But you discovered folk music and the rest is history. Ms. Brico, your piano teacher and a renowned pianist and conductor, thought you made a huge mistake. She said you could have 'gone places.' Recently, you helped documentary film director Jill Godmilo pay tribute to Brico's life in *Antonia: A Portrait of a Woman*. Here's my question: Was she right? Where do you think you would have been as a concert pianist?"

The van turned silent. I looked into Judy Collins' eyes, no longer dangerously blue but warm and pleasant. She smiled, and for the next fifteen minutes she paid tribute to the woman who had given her a gift much larger than the size or color of her eyes. Sometimes, a teacher's best lesson is the one that teaches us to be ourselves.

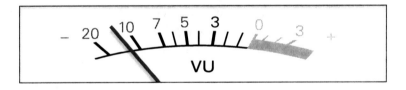

THIRTEEN

Playgirl

I have worked as a DJ for two of America's broadcasting pioneers: The McClendon Corporation and Taft Broadcasting. When I was sharpening my spurs on their maverick hides, I had no sense of their importance in the history of radio or of my future in it. I simply saw the arrangement as worker and capitalism. I was a college student reading too much *Wealth of Nations* and *Das Kapital*. Compared to today's rapacious radio groups, both corporations were as peace loving and generous as Gandhi in a grey flannel suit. We were given turkeys on Thanksgiving and Christmas, stock in the company in lieu of pay raises, and a paid vacation the length of which depended on how many years you had been in bondage … whoops! I mean, how many years you had in service. I didn't appreciate them at the time, but I still have $20 worth of silver dimes that were bestowed on me by "Mother Taft." They are now worth more than $350. And my ten shares of stock were worth $10,000 when I sold them. *Mad Men*'s Don Draper would have been envious.

But DJs, like football coaches, are hired to be fired. My career is littered with questionable decisions. I'm always ready to rely on the truth when any fool, or two-year-old, or two-year-old fool would know better. Shakespearean fools get away with telling the truth. Foolish DJs end up changing their names and moving on to 1,000 watt day-timers in bucolic locales.

An ingenuous excursion into the shifting sands of truth cost me dearly. Yes, I was pretty clueless in my "yoot." It started with a lowly pun.

Cut to the jock lounge in the basement of Q-FM 97, where the topics were poor ratings and sinking the nine ball.

"We need more exposure" suggested John Rivers, our morning jock.

Without missing a beat, I laid my pun on him: "How about a centerfold in *Playgirl*?" Tom Teuber, our music director, groaned and Matt Riedy, our intern, guffawed. "Score one for Santella," I said, rubbing my knuckles on my chest.

Rivers' response was to sink the nine ball and swipe the fifty-cent kitty off the table. "I know an associate editor at *Playgirl*," he said. "I met her when I worked at the 'Loop' (WLUP-AM) in that 'toddling town,' Chicago." Rivers loved his hometown and never tired of telling us how great everything in Chicago was.

What started out as a pun ended up giving four cocky journeymen jocks more exposure then they could handle, but the die was cast. Rivers, Riedy, Teuber, and I were about to embark on an adventure more mythic than *The Lord of the Rings*.

What should have happened next was a couple more games of nine ball with me winning a few shiny quarters. I didn't win any quarters, shiny or otherwise. I lost three straight games distracted by Rivers' comment. "You really know someone at *Playgirl*? It would be a great publicity stunt," I added eagerly.

Rivers sank another nine ball, winked, and quipped, "Can't beat the exposure." By the time I lost my last quarter, Rivers and I were committed to "checking out" the soft porn magazine.

Three days later, as I got ready to start my midday shift, Rivers dropped the bomb. "*Playgirl* is interested in seeing our 'naughty bits.' My friend Suzanne called to say that she might find space in the summer issue if we could get a professional looking portfolio together." Rivers cheeks glowed as red as his beard.

"Do you think we can measure up?" I slapped him with the log.

Every time I asked a jock if they were interested, they answered in the affirmative, followed up by a ribald pun:

She was only the mortician's daughter but any one cadaver.

Or

She was only the telegrapher's daughter but she did-it-did-it-did-it.

Or

She was only the rancher's daughter but all the horsemanure.

Tom Teuber, Matt Riedy, Jim Santella, and John Rivers.

Actually, I made up these daughter puns because I can't repeat the original X-rated material. Even the morning newswoman, Mary van Vorst, agreed to show up ... fully clothed.

Mickey Osterreicher, a newspaper photographer friend of mine, agreed to put together the portfolio for us. The plan was to take the photos in the Q-FM 97 main studio following my Sunday shift, which started at midnight.

Rivers arrived first, followed by Riedy and Teuber. That was it. No one else showed up. We were about to bag the photo shoot when we manned up, decided to shrink the size of the group and proceeded to get down to the nitty-gritty. It was hard to feel comfortable in the studio with four nude jocks hiding coyly behind station t-shirts.

Rivers had no such qualms, though.

It took us less than eight uncomfortable minutes. There was a huge poster of Bob Dylan looking askance and disapprovingly at our antics. We grinned sheepishly, made off-putting remarks, and breathed a sigh of relief when Mickey uttered the four words that we didn't know we were aching to hear. "That's a wrap, gentleman!"

The next morning, the embarrassment of the midnight adventure faded into chest beating bravado. I couldn't wait for my shift to end so I could

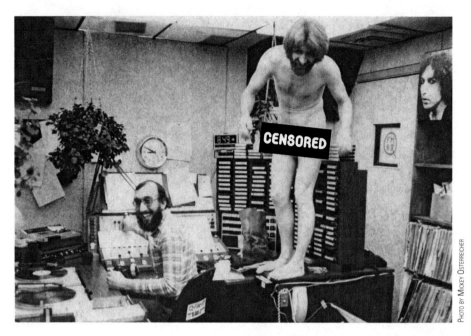

Rivers had no such qualms.

share our daring promotion with the rest of the staff … the competition … the entire radio world! I was stunned by our program director, John McGhan's terse dismissal. "Are you nuts?" It never occurred to me that our brilliant scheme had no place in a radio corporation that considered itself family-oriented.

"But I told you about it," was all I could utter.

"I thought it was a joke, not an invitation to a mass firing. Get rid of those pictures, and from now on keep your promotional ideas unexposed."

The four of us took a lot of flak for boldness. But would you believe the sleeping dog was ready to wake up? Within four months Rivers, Teuber, and Riedy had moved on to better jobs, and Rivers and I decided to send the tainted photos onward and upward to *Playgirl*.

The plan was to put the blame on Rivers and I would plead innocence. How many copies of this soft porn 'zine could there be in Buffalo? A dozen? I misjudged the power of the fifth estate. *The Buffalo News* got a copy of the issue, called station manager Bill Irwin, and got a half-page spread. Not only that, but the Taft national program director, Carl Wagner, just happened to be in Buffalo for his annual tour of the affiliates. I was the only remaining member of the gang of four still employed by Taft. By this time, I was doing mornings and was notified that Carl was in the building and wanted to talk to me.

It was a hot, muggy Monday morning in August 1977 and I was wearing cut-offs. Short cut-offs. How short? Let's put it this way, anyone could tell I was wearing Hanes briefs. It was not the outfit to wear to an interview, especially one as ominous as the upcoming interrogation. As soon as I got off the air, I ran down Allen Street to a men's shop and bought a leather belt, pants, tie and pin-striped shirt. At least I'd be properly dressed for my beheading.

Wagner began: "Jim, I only have three questions for you. Why do you think you are here? What do you have to do with it? And what do you think we should do?" Not only did he want to chop my head off but he wanted me to swing the axe.

I explained the photo session omitting the part about my involvement in it. "Rivers must have sent them to *Playgirl*. He was the only one who had the photos."

"What about the photographer?

"He was a friend of John's."

"What do you think we should do?"

By this time I was mentally packing my bags, ready to find an overnight shift in Cucamonga, California. I had nothing to lose, which prompted me to answer: "Give me a raise for all the free publicity the station has received."

"I don't think we can do that." I played my only trump card.

"Well, somebody has to take the fall, and since I'm the only one of the four jocks left, I guess it's me." I quickly added, "But if you ask anyone who knows me, I work almost ten hours every day and volunteer for every station promotion, whether it pays or not. So, that is not a good solution either. Perhaps a ten-day vacation without pay would work."

I remember the look on Carl's face. "What stones this kid has," it seemed to say. "As of right now, you're no longer employed by Taft. McGhan will officially notify you of your status."

That was it. Once again I played loose and easy with the rules and came up on the short end of the stick. Fortunately, my mom never found out. When my wife, Mary Lou, eventually saw it after years of talk, her response was a blasé, "No big thing."

By the way, later that day I got a call from McGhan. "Don't come to work tomorrow. You're on a two-week vacation. Without pay."

Sex and Stones

Jagger wore red vinyl plastic pants. Keith wore a white linen sport coat. They both exuded rampant sexuality. Rhythm mates Bill Wyman and Charlie Watts were too cool to bat an eye, come hell or high water.

I remember vividly my up close and personal encounter with the Stones. It was the Fourth of July at Summerfest 1978, and the Rolling "F***ing" Stones were preaching to a choir of 80,000 screaming believers at Buffalo's Rich Stadium.

Before the day was over, adulation would turn to intoxicated rage as the world's greatest rock 'n' roll band teetered musically between apotheosis and the apocalypse. Their refusal to play an encore ended in chaos. But let me start at the beginning. Journey, April Wine, and the Atlanta Rhythm Section—the warm-up acts, performed heroically, and the roadies were setting the stage for what would turn into a free for all.

I was back stage standing next to a waiting Mick Jagger, trying to look cool. I touched the brim of my cowboy hat. He smiled slightly and walked toward Keith Richards, who had his spidery long fingers wrapped around the fret board of his guitar.

I'm not sure either one of them really saw me, but I saw them. The moment lasted no more than two seconds. For me, it was an eternity. The road manager quickly gestured me off the stage. The show was about to begin. My fleeting encounter with rock royalty was over. I gave Bill Wyman a thumbs up as he passed me on the backstage stairs. Earlier, I had spent several precious minutes talking to him in the hospitality area, filled to overflowing with world class beautiful women and groaning boards of gourmet food.

What was it like to be close enough to the bad boys of rock to be engulfed by their pheromones? I felt as though I was at the summit of Mount Olympus mingling with the gods. It was unbelievable, dangerous, and decadent. The prince of darkness's labial appendages, immortalized by Andy's Warhol's graphic masterpiece, filled the stage. Before the end of the day, chaos would reign.

It was the Stones' 1978 Tour of the Americas. They were flogging their new album *Some Girls*, released on June 9. The very next day, the road warriors were out on a summer tour to promote it. Buffalo's Summerfest, the Stones third stadium show, was the best of the entire tour.

However, a long wait for the Stones to take the stage, too much alcohol, too little control, and 80,000 Fourth of July partiers created a witch's brew of pandemonium that proved to be incendiary. At one point, Jagger asked the crowd to please not throw bottles at Keith as he sang "Happy" … Things were that wild.

The concert was very short. Worse yet, the band did not play classics like "Gimme Shelter," "Sympathy for the Devil," "Street Fighting Man," "You Can't Always Get What You Want," "Midnight Rambler," "Get Off of My Cloud," etc.

The general consensus was that this was the rowdiest, most dangerous crowd of the entire tour. When the Rolling Stones refused to do an encore, the crowd trashed the stage with garbage, beer bottles, and anything else that wasn't nailed down.

In retrospect, the Stones were in no condition to play a major tour— they were drunk and sloppy, missing chord changes and ending the songs in discord rather than in harmony. But ultimately, *it was only rock 'n' roll* and I loved it.

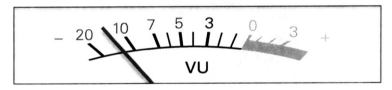

FOURTEEN

Buffalo Bar Crawl

Come along with me as I re-create a 1970s Buffalo bar crawl. We'll begin north of the city, move on to Cheektowaga, then hit the Elmwood strip, Allentown, and downtown Buffalo before finishing by going south to ski country. It may be a bit erratic, like a drunk trying to walk the line, but you'll get the idea. It's an opportunity to drink 'til you drop, without suffering a hangover. This chapter is my tribute to a great city.

In working class Buffalo, booze, blues, bars, and rock go together as effortlessly as Anchor Bar chicken wings and Bocce Club pizza—two staples of my homegrown food and entertainment mecca. I have never felt compelled to seek out greener pastures as a radio nomad because I've always been treated like a hero in my hometown.

So, hop on the magic bus that will take you on a bar crawl of Buffalo's local music scene, as I remember it.

The population of the Buffalo area—1.3 million at one time—provided plenty of drinking patrons. Last call in the Nickel City is 4 a.m. This is often attributed to the historically high density of industrial facilities and the demand by second- and third-shift workers for a beer after work, no matter the time of day or night.

During the '60s, '70s, and beyond, the drinking age in Buffalo was a free-wheeling eighteen. Few of us waited even that long. At sixteen, most of us were toting doctored IDs. My six-foot-two-inch basketball buddy, Joey Ramuda, had a great jump shot, a low IQ, and was artistically blessed. For five bucks he would work his magic on your birth certificate, driver's license, or bus card, adding two years to your age.

Mr. Sartorial Splendor at Mr. Goodbar in the late 1970s.

From rowdy South Buffalo Irish bars like McBride's to Kaisertown's drinking emporiums, young rock wannabes honed their music skills on must-party weekends. Showcase clubs had intimate stages that put customers and musicians within arm's reach of each other. The clubs were also within reach—most destinations were less than a twenty-minute drive away.

So, where shall we start our bar crawl? How about Harvey and Corky's Stage One, way out at Main and Transit? At Stage One, I saw every notable local band, from Two Hills and Actor, to Cock Robin and John "Dr. Dirty" Valby, not to mention touring bands like U2, which opened for Talas on their first American tour. Every Buffalo band wanted to get on that legendary stage and rock. You could hear Talas there most weekends; the trio's stacks of Marshall amps guaranteed an aural bombardment. Female fans crowded the stage to lend their "band-aid" support to the group that began as The Tweeds.

Incredibly, Talas had one regional hit as thirteen-year-old rock marvels who never made it to the "Show." Despite tours opening for Van Halen, they never captured that lightning in a bottle again. Years later, that success would belong to Ani DiFranco and the Goo Goo Dolls. I remember seeing Ani at the tender age of fourteen at the Tralf with an acoustic guitar that dwarfed the diminutive teenager. I was reviewing her concert for *The Buffalo News*, and there was no doubt in my mind that she was something special.

I ran the sound booth at Stage One, playing the music at ear bleeding levels. One of my favorite gimmicks to entertain the crowd was to invite a female patron to come up on stage with me and share half a dozen shots of schnapps. We toasted the band, the bartenders, her boyfriend, the roadies, and her. The trick was, I was drinking water and she was drinking schnapps. One night, though, a new bartender filled my glasses with schnapps, too. I was trapped! Six shots later we were both toasted.

Other headliners at the showcase club included The Police, the Allman Brothers, The Ramones, Judas Priest, and even Aerosmith. They played under the name of Dr. J. Jones and the Interns, giving the Billboard chart busters an opportunity to play to a small club audience like they did back when they got their start in Boston bars. Funny how fledgling rock stars yearn to play to arena size audiences, but when they get that popular, they yearn to return to the intimacy of small clubs.

There was seldom any trouble with the crowds at most of the clubs. Hans, the doorman at Stage One, was one of those no nonsense bouncers. He checked your ID and took the two dollar admission charge. At six feet four and 280 pounds, he could have played nose guard for the Buffalo Bills. He made the ladies feel safe and intimidated the rowdies. One night he shared with me his three-step philosophy: don't drink on the job, don't admit troublemakers, and keep all patrons physically at arm's length.

You could catch the first set at Stage One, which started about 10:30 p.m., and forty-five minutes later it was time to move on to Uncle Sam's in Cheektowaga, where the dance floor alone was the size of Rhode Island. Local bands needed a huge fan base to fill it up, but national acts like the Pretenders thrived in the dance-friendly space. I saw a heavily mascaraed Chrissie Hynde of the Pretenders in 1980 with raccoon eyes and a blown out pixie cut sing an inspired "Back on the Chain Gang," "Brass in Pocket," and "Don't Get Me Wrong" that packed the dance floor.

Time to move into the city. We'll make a brief stop at The Barrel Head in West Seneca and then head downtown. I loved The Barrel Head because it was a ladies' bar—girls adored the spandex-clad bands that played there. Where else would a guy want to be?

Next stop, the Elmwood strip. At one time, numerous corner gin joints sprang up around the South Buffalo steel mills, automobile factories, and grain mills, but with the demise of the industrial north, Buffalo nightlife started forming around college and entertainment districts. In some neighborhoods, every other building was a bar. For instance, students at Buffalo State College, located on the West Side, could have a draft beer at Cole's and literally take six steps into Mr. Goodbar next door. Half a block away from the college, The Royal Pheasant, The Masthead, and Binky Brown's rocked until the wee hours of the morning. Buffalo's 4 a.m. closing time provided ample time to party. And breakfast at 4:30 a.m. at the Towne Restaurant wasn't bad either.

Hop back on our magic bus and it's just a couple of miles down Elmwood to Allentown. From Elmwood and Allen you're within walking distance of Nietzsche's, The Pink, and Mulligan's Brick Bar, ready to score a musical hat trick. Peter, the doorman at Nietzsche's, had a fantastic memory, greeting regulars by name—yours truly included. He'd always manage to find an empty bar stool for me next to the sound booth, the best seat in the long narrow room.

Almost anything and everything happened at Nietzsche's. One night, I caught Chicago blues man, James "Super Harp" Cotton, playing the definitive version of T-Bone Walker's "Stormy Monday," evoking the spirit of Chicago's South Side blues clubs. It's a night I'll never forget.

Across the street from Nietzsche's, Mulligan's Brick Bar bragged the friendliest bartenders, cheapest prices in Allentown, and two dart boards. It was the atmosphere, though, not the music, that made the Brick Bar so popular.

Leaving the Allentown district, let's make a few more stops in downtown Buffalo before we head out to ski country and the Belle Starr in Colden, New York. It's one of the few Western New York areas that you can't reach in twenty minutes.

During the 1970s, and '80s, punk bands like Pauline and the Perils, The Fems, Mark Freeland's Electroman, and The Jumpers lit up The Continental on Franklin, a club that not only embraced stripped-down music but was probably responsible for the sale of more hair products, dyes and style gels than Clairol, L'Oreal, and Toni home permanents combined. But it was the spontaneous revitalizations of rock 'n' roll's ABCs that distinguished the music, the inky-black club, and the musicians who inhabited it.

Pauline was like a pogo stick, constantly jumping from one side of the stage to the other with "I Don't Need You Now." I was smitten! The Fems were a legendary Buffalo hardcore band of the '80s. They self-released 500 copies of "Go to a Party." Nowadays, that single sells for about $400 on eBay. The outrageous name of the group gives you some idea of the band's take no prisoners, hard-core style.

To know Mark Freeland was to be in the company of true genius. Why he was never elevated to the pantheon of immortals is beyond me. I remember Mark sitting in with Dave Constantino, Billy Sheehan, and Paul Varga at Stage One and the result was mystic. Check out "True Love" and "Cathy's Song." He passed away in 2007, too young, too talented, and too outrageous to have been a mere mortal.

Two great Buffalo blues bars are next on the tour: The Belle Starr and the Lafayette Tap Room. Myra Maybelle Shirley Reed Starr, better known as Belle Starr, was a notorious female American outlaw who shares her name with a Swiss chalet-style bar deep in the snowbelt, south of the city.

From its opening in the late 1960s until a fire claimed the building in 1981, it had a reputation for being a rough and tumble roadhouse, drawing authentic blues performers like Muddy Waters, as well as white blues rockers like Stevie Ray Vaughn. From the second floor balcony, customers were close enough to the stage to be able to pick the musicians pockets.

On the other hand, the Lafayette Tap Room was as straight as an arrow—something like 30 feet wide by 140 feet deep. But it was the real deal, booking every major blues legend, from Chicago blues harpist Carey Bell to Buddy Guy and Pinetop Perkins. The first time I saw

Pinetop, he was in his eighties and as fragile as a Kleenex tissue, but he played piano like a tsunami. Ten years later, he was still touring with multitalented Buffalo blues and jazz guitarist Tommy Z.

Our bar crawl ends at another legendary blues bar, The Hideaway, on Delavan across from the Chevy plant, and with our most original favorite son, one who exemplifies the spirit and sound of working class citizens: Stan Szelest.

Like Chicago, New Orleans, Kansas City, Memphis, and Detroit, Buffalo relies on the blues, R&B, jazz, and rock for inspiration. The Buffalo sound itself resides in the connections among The Hideaway, The Rising Sons, and Raven, generated by Stan Szelest, the father of Buffalo blues and R&B.

In 1958, Szelest formed Stan and the Ravens. Two years later, at the age of seventeen, he started working with Ronnie Hawkins and his back-up band, The Hawks. Calling Szelest "a living fountain of rock 'n' roll piano—a one-of-a-kind player," Hawks' bass player, Rick Danko, said he developed his bass style by copying Szelest's left hand. When Szelest left The Hawks, they went on to form a group of their own: The Band.

I saw Stan and the Ravens at The Hideaway. I loved the drummer, Buffalo's own Gary Mallaber, who would go on to play with Raven, ending up as an in-demand studio session player with Steve Miller (*Fly Like an Eagle*), Van Morrison (*Moondance*), and Eddie Money (*Two Tickets to Paradise*). At the time, I was a jazz drummer and went to The Hideaway to check out the young phenomenon. I wasn't impressed initially. I could play that, I thought every time he played a fill, rim shot, or cymbal crash. Eventually, it dawned on me, "This kid is rock solid, never overplays." He was a perfect pocket player. Years later when I told him about the incident, he smiled. I guess I wasn't the only drummer who had underestimated the superlative studio player.

When Stan and the Ravens broke up, Mallaber and bass player Tommy Calandra joined the Rising Sons, which eventually included singer Tony Galla. In 1968, with J. R. Weitz on guitar and Jimmy Calire on keyboards, they became Raven, were signed up by Columbia Records, and scored a breakout self-titled LP. Raven frequently played after hours with the likes of Jimi Hendrix and The Doors at Steve Paul's popular New York City club, The Scene. When Columbia did not renew their contract, the band split up. From Stan and the Ravens to the Rising Sons to Raven, the history of 1960s and 1970s bands in Buffalo is a tale of close but no cigar.

It's last call. Tip your bartender and make your last one for the road a soft drink.

As Dragnet's Joe Friday might intone, "The preceding individuals and drinking institutions represent just a small sample" of the talented musicians that made Buffalo special to me. It was our time. Our music. Our city. Our destiny.

A complete list of Buffalo bars and bands would fill an encyclopedia. Did your favorites make the list? Fill in the blanks.

Bars

After Dark	Aliotta's	
		The Barrel Head
Beef and Ale	Belle Starr	
Binky Brown's	Bona Vista	Brick Bar
	Club 2000	Cole's
	The Continental	Doolittle's Sky Room
Gabel's	Gabriel's Gate	
He and She's		The Hideaway
	The Inferno	
Lafayette Tap Room	Lulu Belle's	The Masthead
McVan's		Mean Guys East
	Melanie's	
		Mickey Rats
The Mohawk	Mulligan's	
	Nietzsche's	
		Patrick Henry's
The Pink		Play Boy Club
The Poor House	Rooftop's	
Salty Dog		Stage One
	Uncle Sam's	

Bands

	Big Wheelie & the Hubcaps	
Cheater	Cock Robin	
	Fare Trade	The Fems
Gamalon		George Doran
	Harpo	Jambo
Jesse Galante	The Jumpers	
		Pauline & the Perils
Pegasus		
	Raven	The Road
	Rodan	
Stan Szelest		
	Talas	
Two Hills		Week End

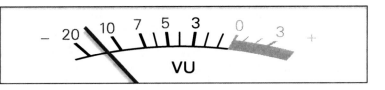

FIFTEEN

WUWU

In 1981, Lady Luck blew on my dice again. I was hired to program a start-up station that went by the unlikely call letters WUWU-FM, affectionately known as "Woo–Woo." It was raw, chancy, and almost as exciting as my first days in radio. One of radio's bona fide maniacs, Bob Allen, convinced dentist Dr. Ronald Chmiel, known around the station as "Dr. Tooth," to bankroll the radio station.

The first few months we were on the air, we had to drive twenty-two miles from Buffalo to Wethersfield and climb a ladder to a loft to broadcast from our transmitter shack. All the shack contained was transmitter equipment, a bathroom with a nonworking sink, and a desk that held a broadcast board, two turntables, and a microphone. There were so many missing planks and supports that the buzzing bees and chirping barn swallows flitted easily in and out of the ramshackle building. Cows mooed outside. When it rained, the roof leaked. It was warmed by a small electric space heater. With several boxes of LPs, we'd put the woo in WUWU.

Eventually, we moved to permanent studios on Clinton Street in West Seneca and kept afloat until 1983. We played everything from techno pop to Led Zeppelin, The Clash to The Beatles, The Sex Pistols to Lou Reed. The Fugs might be paired with Joni Mitchell, followed by Judas Priest, which in turn might be followed by Frank Zappa or Emerson, Lake, and Palmer. It was musical anarchy. It was undisciplined. It was great! The first day we broadcast "Psycho Chicken" by The Fools for twenty-four hours straight without interruption.

There are those who will tell you that WUWU was the most exciting music station ever to be heard in Buffalo. There's an even larger number of people who will swear that the station was populated by annoying brats who had no business being trusted with a radio license. It was glorious mayhem. It was legendary. Not a day went by without a major crisis.

Let me set the scene for you. Cars, ships, planes, and even trains have been known to be hijacked, but not radio towers. I was driving my pride and joy, a late model red MGB to WUWU, unaware of the on-air adventure that lay ahead of me that day. Little did I know it was a day that would go down in Buffalo radio history.

My MGB was the sport car *du jour*, with bucket seats that put my butt less than eighteen inches from the road. When I passed American gas guzzlers, I could see my reflection in their hub caps. My short was holding the road like the Silver Surfer catching a monster wave—definitely tubular. I was on my way to our wacky-weed radio station where the rules were: "There are no rules!" I was the program director, I had pulled the afternoon drive shift, and I was taking up the slack left when station manager Bob Allen, a true mad man, was let go after a brouhaha with Dr. Tooth. When I signed on to run the asylum, I predicted a life expectancy of six months. We were in our second year of benign chaos. Bob was a loony of the first order with a passion for radio that matched mine. I liked him despite the warts.

May 21, 1983, was a gorgeous day. The staff was cozily ensconced in our West Seneca studios enjoying the air conditioning. The eighty degree temperature was making a liar of Johnny Carson's cheap shots about Buffalo weather. With the Blizzard of '77, Buffalo got to be a national joke. Johnny Carson made a living exaggerating our annual snowfall, but if the Buffalo Bills couldn't impress the nation with four Super Bowl appearances, we made *The Tonight Show* with our snowfall. To retaliate I had started making up cheap shots about Californians. "Why are Californians like granola? What's not fruits or flakes are nuts." Over the years, I sent Carson many jokes. None of them ever made it into his monologues.

As I walked into the WUWU production studio that day, Jeff Gordon, my morning guy, was taping a few promos for his show *Leave It To Teddy* (his alter ego) and *Franklin's Furnace* (Bob's edgy talk show). We had a motley crew. "The Unknown DJ," our all-night jock, was earning his wings as a teenage radio rookie. There was Bill Nichols, who did weekends with his cat, Wizard. We called them The Dynamic Duo.

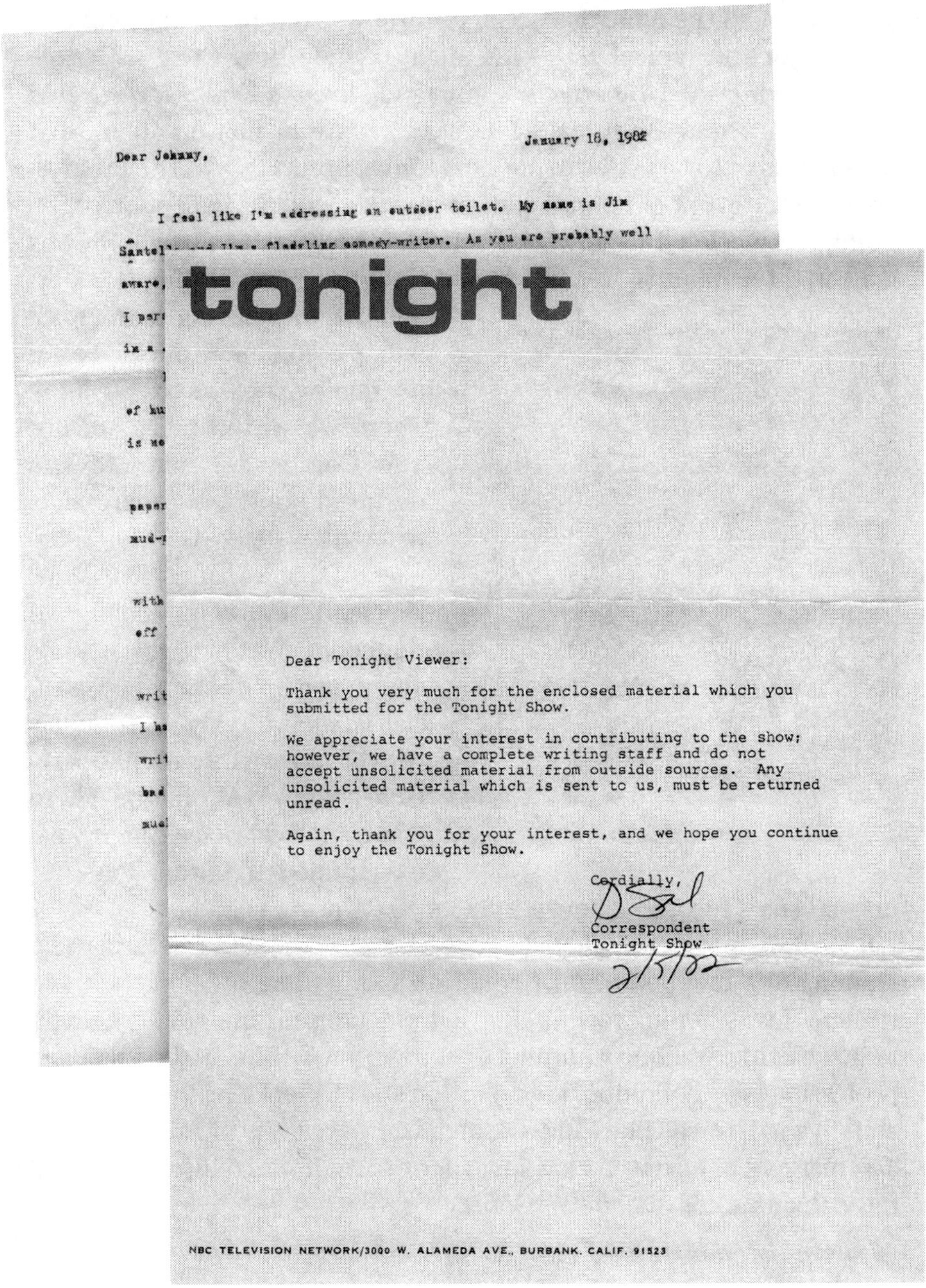

January 18, 1982

Dear Johnny,

I feel like I'm addressing an outdoor toilet. My name is Jim
Santel... ...and Jim a fledgling comedy-writer. As you are probably well
aware,

I per...
in a...

of hu...
is me...

paper...
mud-...

with...
off...

wri...
I ha...
wri...
had...
mus...

tonight

Dear Tonight Viewer:

Thank you very much for the enclosed material which you
submitted for the Tonight Show.

We appreciate your interest in contributing to the show;
however, we have a complete writing staff and do not
accept unsolicited material from outside sources. Any
unsolicited material which is sent to us, must be returned
unread.

Again, thank you for your interest, and we hope you continue
to enjoy the Tonight Show.

Cordially,

Correspondent
Tonight Show

2/5/82

NBC TELEVISION NETWORK/3000 W. ALAMEDA AVE., BURBANK, CALIF. 91523

Here's one of my favorites: "The Secretary of Agriculture has just announced a breakthrough in the poultry industry. It's the Republican turkey complete with two right wings."

The cat got all the funny lines. Gary Storm was our music director and midday jock. A typical set of his might include Bing Crosby, George Jones, the Mormon Tabernacle Choir, and Mozart's *Eine Kleine Nacht Musik*. Gary was a musical egalitarian. He never met an album that didn't deserve to be added to our burgeoning library. We were a progressive, freeform, out-of-control staff of lunatics with the exception of Les Trent, our weekend jock, who was destined to outshine us all. He was gone in three months. He ended up at *Entertainment Tonight*.

In the WUWU studio.

Me, I was having a freeform ball playing new music based on quality, not chart position. There was a ton of it. Locally, The Continental and McVan's nurtured punk and progressive. Brits like Peter Gabriel influenced Buffalo bands like Mark Freeland's Pegasus, Rodan, and Gamalon. We had no qualms about pairing techno pop with classic rock, Muddy Waters blues with progressive music like early Genesis and Marillion. There was even West Coast Americana, exemplified by Gram Parsons, one of Gary's favorite country, influenced California bands.

It was a high water mark, but I knew that our days as a freeform radio station were numbered. All I could do was update my air-check and resumé. I was hoping for the best but planning for the worst. Being a radio DJ is like walking a burning tight rope; you're hired to be fired. The profession is by definition nomadic. You start by working the graveyard shift in small towns like Enid, Oklahoma, peak at one of America's Top Ten markets like New York, Chicago, or L. A., if you're lucky, and end up as the morning man on W*O*L*D.

*I am the morning DJ on W*O*L*D*
Playing all the hits for you wherever you may be
The bright good-morning voice who's heard but never seen
Feeling all of forty-five going on fifteen
The drinking I did on my last big gig made my voice go low
They said that they liked the younger sound when they let me go

So I drifted on down to Tulsa, Oklahoma, to do me a late
night talk show
Now I worked my way back home again, via Boise, Idaho
That's how this business goes.

(Harry Chapin, *W*O*L*D*)

Back to my story. I had a great "radio" set planned for my show on
that lovely day in May:

1. *FM*	Steely Dan
2. *Radio, Radio*	Elvis Costello
3. *Radio Clash*	The Clash
4. *Mexican Radio*	Wall of Voodoo
5. *Clap for the Wolfman*	Guess Who
6. *Heard it on The X*	ZZ Top

The "radio" set never made it on the air. I started my show:

"Jim Santella with you on WUWU. Put your hand on the radio as we
enter the Church of the Holy Rock and Rollers. For the next four hours,
you are invited to celebrate America's gift to teenage spirit, the radio!
Here's a sample of what you can expect—Steely Dan with the title song
from their *FM* album."

I fired up the remote start on the turntable, and while the music was
playing I loaded a Mighty Taco spot and started prereading the live
copy for a PSA. I heard a crackling sound in my headphones followed
by dead air. I started dialing up the telemetry that connected the West
Seneca studios with the Wethersfield transmitter. Suddenly a nasally
voice jumped out of the speakers.

> "On Saturday May 21, 1983, Dr. Ronald A. Chmiel, a Cheek-
> towaga dentist who happens to be a stockholder of Seven Star
> Stereo Inc., without the authority of the board of directors, ille-
> gally attempted to fire me, and since that time he's been running
> an unauthorized and illegal radio station."

It was Bob Allen. Like Lazarus risen from the dead, the former general
manager was alive and broadcasting from the transmitter shack.

> "Dentist Chmiel and his son Ron Jr., during the past ten days,
> have been working to change the format of WUWU-FM, includ-
> ing the removal of records from the record library that they
> think should not be played. Last week an unauthorized memo

was handed out by Chmiel Jr. telling employees what music to play and what not to play before they purged the music library."

I couldn't believe it. I plopped my head on the broadcast board and listened to the madman.

"… The station has been breaking Federal Communications Commission rules all week including illegal station IDs, not broadcasting station IDs, plus broadcasting profanity during daytime hours when children, business establishments, and people who want to enjoy quality entertainment without profanity and obscenities are listening. The changes in the musical format of WUWU this week are making listeners complain and is noticeable. However, on the air, the announcers are denying it. Perhaps they have orders from the dentist."

I started laughing. It was simply too funny to do anything else. WUWU was being hijacked. The only thing missing was a pirate ship, a skull and crossbones flag, and Bob Allen with an eye patch and a wooden leg. It was a WOO-WOO moment. It was even more outrageous than when I walked off the air eleven years earlier. I quickly called the staff together to take advantage of the circus-like events that were sure to ensue. I gave the troops their marching orders. "I will field all questions from the media. It's show time and Bob Allen, Dr. Tooth, and WOO-WOO are the main attraction! Let's not get in the way. We have a rendezvous with the news media."

"… Ladies and gentlemen, this is no promotion. An illegal takeover unauthorized by the authority that runs our radio station, the board of directors, has taken place. I am Robert Allen … I am going to court and filing a major lawsuit on behalf of the stock holders. We have taken over the transmitters of WUWU, legally, and notified the Federal Communications Commission of this."

Meanwhile, at crosstown rival 97 Rock, production director Jim Pastrick was monitoring WUWU and performing equipment maintenance. Without missing a beat, he flipped the studio tape machine into record mode, capturing the event for posterity and yours truly.

Throughout the day, I conducted live interviews with stations across the country as well as Canada. Everything culminated with a Channel 2 TV female reporter (name deleted to protect the innocent). Her off-camera questions assured me that the broadcast would be flattering for the

I just love my fans. Affectionately drawn by "Tina Peel" in 1982.

station. The opening logo segued to the anchor, *"Taking you out to West Seneca where radio station WUWU is currently being held hostage. Channel 2 with breaking news."*

Instead of tossing up a softball question, however, the street reporter whistled a fastball past my ears. "Recently dismissed general manager Bob Allen has hijacked WOO-WOO's transmitter. Jim, is he crazy?"

How do you answer that? It's like being asked if you "still beat your wife?" I knew Bob was listening and was just nuts enough to sue for slander. I blinked, cleared my throat and replied "Some people might say so." I took the sting out of the knockdown pitch.

The remaining twenty-five seconds were a blur. The reporter gave me a thumb's up as she and her cameraman packed up the equipment. "Nice answer."

There was one more small incident: I got a call around 10 p.m. from the state police notifying me that Mr. Allen had been removed from WUWU's radio transmitter shack. I had music tracking on all day, so I knew exactly when the West Seneca studio went back on air. By that time, the evening DJ, the cleaning lady, and I were the only ones left in the building. As I walked out of the station, I noticed a rusty station wagon in the parking lot. It was Bob Allen. I walked toward the vehicle, cautiously. It could have been a scene out of *Play Misty for Me* or *Talk Radio*. Both movies end with homicides.

The car door opened and Bob stepped out. I grasped my coffee thermos just a tad tighter. "Hi, big fellow," I said with a big shit-eating grin. "Did we have fun, today?"

His reply was precious. "Do you think we put the fear of God in those mother-f**kers?" We both laughed. That was the last time I ever saw Bob Allen.

The next day, I was called into Doctor Tooth's office. He praised my handling of the tower takeover and asked who I thought might fill the general manager's position. I gave him a short list of three candidates. I cautioned him not to hire WBLK's production director.

He'd been hanging around our station and everyone knew he was gunning for the job. I felt he knew nothing about progressive radio and would probably turn WUWU into a dance format if hired. It was déjà vu all over again. He was hired, I was fired, and within ninety days the new dance format was declared a disaster.

With the end of WUWU, I felt I had come full circle in freeform rock 'n' roll radio. For the next five years, I devoted my time to completing my master's degree.

III

JACK OF ALL TRADES

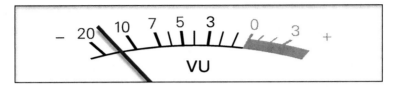

SIXTEEN

Back to School and Beyond

loved high school. My four year high school average was ninety-four percent. That included such brain-breakers as typing, office machinery, accounting, and business math. Who knows if I was ready for college, but I was the first person in my family to make the attempt.

On a lovely autumn day in September 1956, I enrolled in UB as a bright-eyed, bushy-tailed freshman, complete with a blue beanie, five registration cards, and fifty pounds of textbooks (not one e-book).

I finally earned my master's degree—yes, I have a master's degree. It took me thirty-two years from that September day to the day they put the diploma in my hand. I managed to accumulate 244 academic credit hours over those years, and I still have the official transcript to prove it.

What does a DJ do when he is too old to rock 'n' roll and too young to die? Answer: Go back to school. Whether I quit my on-air radio job or was tossed out for boogieing away my scruples, I enrolled in a college course, ostensibly to expand my mind. I gathered a boatload of arcane facts and talking points between 1956 and 1988 as I majored in every discipline from accounting to history, from music to theater. When I first started at WBFO in 1967, I was already on my third major. I even dropped out of film studies, which consisted of simply watching movies! Five years after leaving WUWU, I finally graduated with a B.A. in English and a master's degree in media studies.

Unfortunately, there is no correlation between smarts and entertaining radio. What skills do you need to succeed as a broadcaster? I assure you that you'll need substantially less than a butcher, a baker, or a candlestick maker. I don't claim to be any smarter than your common variety book worm or Top 40 jock, but I do have a passion for education.

Being a DJ is not a lifelong career. The goal of disc jockeys is to be on the air. Most jocks spend half of their working life trying to get on the air. Once they get on the air, they spend half their lives trying to figure out how to stay there. After their on air life is over, DJs often go into sales—real estate, radio promotions, automobiles, etc. I don't know any jocks who retired from radio with a pension. That includes me.

When you're no longer wanted on the radio, the one thing you want is to stay connected to it. Fortunately, I was able to take my love of music, theater, and film to forge the second half of my career. I ended up going from being a full-time disc jockey to being a factotum—a fancy term for jack of all trades. I worked as a cameraman, grip, photographer, producer, writer. It all started when I got fired from WUWU and decided to go back to school. Everyone always says you need a college education to get a good job. Not me. I was proud of the fact that I was making a good living without a degree. I was working in radio, having fun—why would I want to complete my education? Answer: For myself.

While at WUWU in 1981, I got the bright idea that I wanted to return to music reviewing. I called Dale Anderson of *The Buffalo News* and he suggested I talk to Terry Doran, the *News'* arts editor. Terry said: "The next time you go to a concert, review it and send me a copy." That very night I went to a concert, wrote a review, and had it on his desk the next morning. The rest is history. The opportunity to go to clubs and concert halls to hear music for free was like a dream come true. I reviewed rock, country, pop, classical, blues, you name it. Later on, I also reviewed theater, books, dance, and movies.

I had always wanted to be a writer. I think working at a newspaper is really the best writing experience. You get to be creative on a daily basis. Each assignment offers a new challenge. You learn how to write the review in your head as you're driving to the newsroom from the event to meet the deadline. Completing the writing by midnight was either exciting or nervewracking. Remember, in those days there were no laptops or Internet connections. You had to actually go to the newsroom to write the story. By the late '90s, I did have a modem in my home to replace my battered Royal typewriter.

Since completing my degree was not cheap, working on film crews at Sherwin-Greenberg Productions was a great source of income. I worked on *The Natural*; *Planes, Trains, and Automobiles*; and I even had the good fortune to be on stage within six feet of Bill Clinton when he appeared at Shea's Buffalo during his first presidential run. Only the heavily armed Secret Service men were closer. My predominant memory was watching one of the agents hold onto Clinton's belt as he leaned over the stage to shake hands.

I'd advise you never to send me on shoot that takes place on a boat, though. My stomach can't take it. I can laugh at it now, but the time I was sent out onto Lake Erie to run sound for a commercial, my job had to be taken over by a production assistant, as I got sick over the side of the boat. When we got back to shore, I thought my suffering had ended for the day until the boat captain asked if I was ready to go out again. I thought he was kidding. But by this time, I had nothing left to lose. To this day, even when visiting my brother-in-law, Len, who owns a winery on Keuka Lake, I don't venture onto his boat, no matter how many bottles of wine he bribes me with.

By now, you must have caught on that I've been a frustrated comic since my childhood. Groucho Marx, Woody Allen, and Steve Allen were some of my comic inspirations. Unlike these masters of wit, my style always seemed to border on the silly. I lacked two essential traits to be a successful comedian: an original sense of humor and "timing." Political satirist Mark Russell had loads of both. I was his floor director on WNED's *Mark Russell Comedy Special* for more than twenty years.

Because Mark was so secure working with me, he made sure that as a freelancer I was brought in to be his permanent floor director. I was familiar with all aspects of the production, so I was able to anticipate any possible problems

Floor-directing the Mark Russell show in 2002.

and solve them. I had his back no matter what. I made sure that Mark was comfortable and ready to go on. I acted as preshow buffer between him and enthusiastic fans and made sure he was not distracted during the last thirty minutes before airtime. Mark's stock-in-trade was his ability to put new words to well-known melodies satirizing the headlines of the day. He would refine his show up to the very last minute. Even though there were two rehearsals for the show, more frequently than not he'd ad lib a line or two on some late-breaking news event. I learned a lot just listening to him. It was like going to comedy school. He was such a pro.

Mark was a kind, warm, and genuine human being—and damned funny! Not only that, he was generous. My wife, Mary Lou ("she who must be obeyed"), and I both looked forward to his annual gifts of White House Christmas ornaments. At one point, I thought we were going to need a second Christmas tree. I traveled with that show to Philadelphia, Washington, DC, New Orleans, and Toronto. You can see he also contributed to my frequent flyer miles!

I went on to write and produce quite a few shows for WNED-TV during the late '90s and early 2000s. I am most proud of the *Read to Succeed* promos, four short TV spots designed to encourage kids to read, and several years of *Kids Voting* programs. One of the *Read to Succeed* spots was called "The Reading Rap."

Top: Jim with Mark Russell.
Bottom: Writer-producer at WNED-TV in the early 2000s.

It was fun to work with my wife, Mary Lou, who was an elementary vocal music teacher. Her professional experience as a music theater performer proved invaluable. She taught a group of second and third graders a choreographed rap about how cool reading is. The kids loved it. I even busted a move or two.

I'm not a fan of multitasking. It's a waste of time. Focus on one thing, do it well, and then move on. This is ironic since my life has been filled to overflowing with holding down two and three jobs at a time. In 1988, while still freelancing at Sherwin-Greenberg, I got a call from John Hager, 97 Rock's program director. He asked me to re-create my progressive radio shows of the '60s on an overnight show. John trusted me. I had total freedom to play anything I wanted, including music from my personal collection. I called it Radiation Theater.

WELCOME TO THE THEATER

Drama has always been my passion, Shakespeare my favorite playwright. I love reading, researching, and reviewing plays. I even got to tread the boards. Acting was always a learning experience. It gave me a better understanding of the process.

During the '90s I worked a lot with Neal Radice at the Alleyway Theatre, who often cast me as a dying father figure. It got so that when I auditioned for a role I'd ask, "What scene do I die in?" Neal's frequent advice to me was to take a little space and don't hang your heels on the set. Rehearsals were the best part of acting—getting to develop a character and becoming someone completely different. Staying in character could be a

Treading the boards as the apothecary in *Rattus, Rattus* at Alleyway Theatre.

challenge, however. Once, in a Larry Gray play, as the curtain rose, I lay sick and dying on a couch. Two elderly ladies arriving late clambered to their front row seats no more than ten feet from me. They were oblivious to how distracting the commotion they were creating was. I began my opening speech to my stage wife, Mary Loftus. I went up on my lines, but no matter how much Mary attempted to bring me back to the script, my mind just wouldn't go there. Eventually, she gave up, we skipped a few pages of dialogue, and the show went on. Such is live theater.

On a more pleasant note, I got a chance to meet Kitty Carlisle Hart backstage at the Alleyway. She was the wife of famed playwright Moss Hart. He and his partner George S. Kaufman were two of Broadway's most inventive playwrights. Kaufman was an inveterate "play doctor" and tremendously influenced my writing philosophy. Whenever he got stuck with writer's block, his reaction was to cut all the excessive writing to the bone. Easier said than done, I've found.

Manny Fried, esteemed Buffalo playwright and actor, preached the same lesson. Manny was a voice for the working man, a stalwart individual who faced down McCarthy in the H.U.A.C hearings. He was of the same generation as my dad. They would have loved each other. Manny felt like my surrogate father. I had the privilege of performing with Manny many times, and I took his playwriting class more than a couple of times.

Some of my most satisfying theater work was with the Theater of Youth (T.O.Y.). It is not only important but essential that we introduce children to the magic of the stage as early as possible. Artistic director Meg Quinn has devoted her energy for more than a quarter of a century to this goal. In a production of *The Secret Garden*, I played Ben, the gardener. In one scene in which I was tending the garden, I poked my hoe under a youngster's first row seat and yanked his lunch bag out from under it. His eyes were like saucers. At that moment, I understood Meg's mission.

About this same time I had some plays produced, including a comedy entitled *The Couch*. In the late 1990s, I also wrote the book for a musical revue, a spoof of Irving Berlin's life called *Izzy*. Grant Golden was the composer. It was later revised and produced at MusicalFare in 2001. I'd like to think all of this hands-on experience made me a better theater reviewer.

In 1993, I returned to my first love. No, not Carol, the girl next door— jazz! I grew up on the jazz-infused West Side. Joe Rico, for whom Stan Kenton wrote "Jump for Joe," and Carol Hardy were the jazz DJs I admired most. Their soft-spoken delivery would come to characterize my own radio style. My very first radio program was *Time Out for Jazz*.

And now I was thrilled to get a call from Al Wallack of WEBR-AM, who wanted me for the program *Jazz in the Nighttime*. I got an overnight weekend shift. Nineteen ninety three was also the year I returned to WBFO, not as a paid employee but as a volunteer, on a four-and-a-half-minute show called *Theater Talk* with Anthony Chase, professor at Buffalo State and writer for *Theater Week*. Tony and I also did a review segment on WUTV Channel 29's *Midday*. We discovered we'd been neighbors without knowing it for nearly two years, living right across the street from one another in the University District. Tony loved my mom's baking. She was living with me then. Tony couldn't wait for her homemade rolls, pastries, and at Christmas time, *cuccidati*, the real name of those luscious Sicilian fig cookies.

Talking about sweet things, it was in 1992 that I met my future wife, Mary Lou, a short, spunky music teacher full of energy and smiles. I came to learn she'd gone to dancing school for years with my cousin Corinne Melancon, a Broadway actress, and Mary Lou knew my aunts and uncles and even my Italian-speaking grandmother. Grandma Santella had pinched Mary Lou's cheeks the same way she'd pinched mine!

We met at a party for Corinne, who had come to Buffalo to play the lead in the musical *Grand Hotel* at Shea's. When just a handful of friends remained at the end of the evening, I was headed to Flynn's, the local theater bar. "To be polite," I asked Mary Lou to come along. To my surprise she said okay. "To be polite," I asked for her number. Later that week, "to be polite," I asked her out. When she asked me to marry her four years later, "to be polite," I said, "Yes." See where politeness will get you? We've been happily married for ten years. Ten out of seventeen's not bad.

SEVENTEEN

Santella Claus

Like Superman and Clark Kent, I've always harbored a secret identity. Jim Santella would hide behind his trademark glasses, leather hat, and beard. Santella Claus was identified by his mischievous smile, glistening eyes, cowboy hat, and beard. Like Jimmy Olsen, who knew how to get to Superman, the elves knew how to get Santella Claus to the studio of 97 Rock. Once a year, Santella Claus would visit all the good little boys and girls and distribute musical treats.

I love Christmas. It's my favorite holiday, and while working for 97 Rock, I got to play Santa Claus too. Being single at that time, I didn't have Christmas morning commitments so I would volunteer to work. The legendary six-hour *Santella Claus Christmas Music Marathon* greeted listeners each December 25 from 1991 to 2010, beginning at 97 Rock and ending at WBFO when it was still at UB.

Little did I know that a small touch of generosity from me—volunteering to work on Christmas morning—would become a holiday gift that lasted twenty years.

The show ran from 6 a.m. to noon. I woke so early for that show, I thought that one year I might actually catch Santa sliding down the chimney. Every year I looked for traces of him. My only regret was that no matter how early I woke up, the jolly elf was gone before I could see him. I know there is a Santa Claus because the cookies I leave for him each year are always gone.

Originally, I thought I'd play a few Christmas rock songs like Springsteen's "Santa Claus is Comin' to Town," or AC/DC'S "Mistress for Christmas," mixed with the regular programming and let it go at that. That lasted … about an hour. It turned into a holiday musicfest. No one told me what to do, so I simply chose a variety of tunes and developed the show while other radio stations prerecorded their holiday shows. It's hard to believe, but Santella Claus was one of the first to mix Christmas rock music in with traditional carols.

From the get-go I enjoyed a stroke of luck. When sister station WGR-AM was cleaning house, they offered me a huge collection of carts—single songs recorded on tape. It jump started my collection of traditional holiday tunes. I featured lesser known songs, playing everything from Eartha Kitt's "Santa Baby" to "Father Christmas" by The Kinks.

One of the joys of the *Christmas Music Marathon* was that there was more than just music. I was the only one to incorporate special readings into my holiday show. I recorded some readings for Mary Lou to use in her music classroom during the holidays and they became a part of my show. They included *'Twas the Night Before Christmas*, *The Polar Express*, and *How the Grinch Stole Christmas*, as well as *Yes, Virginia There is a Santa Claus* and *Christmas Cows*. Over the years I've enjoyed sharing these stories with my grandchildren and great nieces and nephews.

For adults there were comedy routines like Cheech and Chong, Stan Freeberg's shopping satire and *The Irish Twelve Days of Christmas*. I played everything from Bing Crosby's "White Christmas" to "Christmas Wrappings" by The Waitresses, and I'd follow "All I Want for Christmas is My Two Front Teeth" with the quirky send-up entitled "All I Want for Christmas is a Beatle."

For a guy who eschewed formats all of his life, I followed a simple mix. It worked—a rock Christmas song, traditional Christmas song, comedy, some fun facts and one reading each hour. There was always something new to discover. Friends, fans, and family called me throughout the morning with requests and thanks. Sometimes, I put them on the air. I think the show had heart. Nowadays, most stations play an endless list of Christmas music without any context.

Christmas trivia abounded. As the years progressed, I really enjoyed adding facts and figures about the history of Christmas, shopping statistics, and the number of cookies consumed by Santa Claus. According to Santella Claus's chief elf accountant, who keeps track of that sort of thing, Santa eats about a billion cookies in one twenty-four-hour trip

With Mary Lou at a WBFO Christmas party in Niagara Falls in 2003.

around the world, not to mention the gazillions of glasses of milk he drinks to wash them down!

Santella Claus still lives in my heart. Who knows? Santella Claus may just come and visit one more time. Remember, as Chris Van Allsburg states in *The Polar Express*: "The bell still rings for those who truly believe."

So keep on believing.

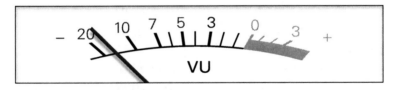

EIGHTEEN

Are You Ready for the Blues?

From 1997 to 2013, I opened my weekend blues shows at WBFO-FM with the provocative question: "Are you ready for the blues?" If my epitaph included just those six words, I would be immensely proud of my brief stay on this "pale blue dot." My later years in Buffalo radio are defined by these six iconic words.

I closed out the final third of my forty-five-year radio career playing America's original music, the blues. On my watch, WBFO became the "Home of the Blues." I wanted my audience to understand the role of the blues in American popular music. My intention was to entertain, to educate, and to elevate.

I am forever grateful for the opportunity to grow a four-hour Saturday afternoon blues show into a ten-hour blues weekend. It all started in 1997. I was still writing for *The Buffalo News*, working at 97 Rock and at WNED-TV. I wasn't making much money, but I sure was working a lot. A few months earlier my stint on the overnight show, *Jazz in the Nighttime* ended when WNED-AM purchased WEBR-AM. So my Saturdays were free.

My musical taste has always been eclectic, so it was no surprise when I got a call from WBFO's music director Bert Gambini telling me the station needed a new blues host. Station manager David Benders offered me the job and I accepted immediately. Dave always said he didn't have to look far for the right guy. I was already there once a week recording *Theater Talk* anyway. Throughout my radio career, I have always been able to choose my own music, and the blues show was no different.

After the show, Dave and I chatted endlessly about music. Well, chatting might be the wrong word; filibustering would be more accurate.

I was disappointed when I found out that my weekend shift was scheduled for Saturdays from 11 a.m. to 3 p.m. rather than at night when blues shows traditionally aired. Blues musicians and blues fans didn't even go to sleep until 11 a.m.! Right?

Boy was I wrong. I learned that my blues audience was not only ready for the blues at those times, they thrived on them. My show accompanied listeners shopping, puttering around the house, working on the lawn, and doing a thousand and one other weekend chores. The blues were the perfect, portable entertainment companion. I would find out how important this was years later.

OOPS! THE WEDDING

My first blues show was scheduled to air on November 22, 1997. There was just one small hitch, I was scheduled to be married the following week. Mary Lou, my wife to be, was less than happy with the timing.

Our wedding reception was marked by two quirky events. First, I discovered I could not dance. Actually, I never could. Mary Lou had spent weeks teaching me a basic fox trot: step-tap-step-tap-step-step-step-tap. As we got on the dance floor, I whispered in her ear: "I can't remember one step," which was not the sweet "I love you" she expected. Worse than that, as the buffet progressed, my lips and face swelled like a pufferfish. Oh my God, was I allergic to Mary Lou? I thought maybe I could get a quick annulment, but my brother-in-law, a doctor, diagnosed it as just a seafood allergy. A quick dose of Benadryl put me on the road to recovery. Actually, it put me on the road to Cleveland and the Rock and Roll Hall of Fame—no way I was going to miss that honeymoon.

A wonderful memory from our reception was Mary Lou's mom, Lorraine, who was eighty-years-old at the time, playing the piano. Mary Lou is a musician, her mom was a musician, and so was her maternal grandfather. Lorraine began playing piano in a dance band with her brothers, The Tepas Junior Band, at the age of ten. By the time we got married, she weighed about a hundred pounds and walked with a cane. Some of our friends wondered what on earth she might sound like, but when she sat down and her fingers touched the keys, she came alive. She played through a medley of tunes and then played requests without ever stopping, segueing from one song to another as Mary Lou's entire family and I stood around the piano and sang. It was an amazing display of talent and tenacity. Her playing was like sipping from the fountain of youth.

The very next night we were walking around a downtown Cleveland square decorated for Christmas. Mary Lou started up a conversation with a holiday Santa Claus, and when he found out that we were on our honeymoon, he arranged a free ride for us in a horse-drawn carriage. It was even more special when I told the driver my name was "Santella Claus," and that Santa and I were related! Believe it or not, it was a lovely, romantic ride—despite the allergy—perfect for the original romantic: me.

GEOGRAPHY IS DESTINY

I've always been fascinated by the connection between the blues and practically every kind of music that the blues spawned. The blues are arguably the most pervasive American music style of the last century and a half. In the rich history of the blues, two overriding principles summarize the development and spread of this unique American music: "Geography is destiny," and the two "Great Migrations" from rural to urban America that followed World War I and World War II.

Geography is destiny, for me, simply means where you are born defines how you sound. For example, bluesmen born and raised along the Mississippi delta were influenced by local acoustic slide guitarists like Charlie Patton, Son House, and Robert Johnson. Professor Longhair ("Roy" Byrd), on the other hand, who was born and raised in

New Orleans, employs twelve-to-the-bar piano rhythms. The ragtime finger-picking style identified with the Piedmont blues of the East Coast was typified by Blind Blake, the Reverend Gary Davis, and Blind Willie McTell.

The two World Wars lured laborers away from the agrarian South to the industrial North where high paying jobs awaited them. Musicians brought their Southern hometown music to Chicago's juke joints where they electrified and amplified it so it could be heard in the noisy, urban bars. Little did anyone dream that the blues would dominate popular music in the twentieth century. As Muddy Waters would later observe, "The blues had a baby and they called it rock 'n' roll."

The blues influenced mainstream song writers from Irving Berlin and George Gershwin, to Bob Dylan and the Beatles. Country, jazz, and even rap fall into that category. Did you know that the theme music for the television series *Batman* is a blues tune? Blues musician Keb' Mo' performed his blues rendition of "America the Beautiful" to close out the final season of *The West Wing*. It's hard to believe that a simple six-note scale, a twelve bar, AAB, three-chord structure supports such a myriad of inventiveness.

As preeminent folk bluesman Lead Belly was fond of saying: "All music is folk music. I ain't never heard no animal playing it." That anecdotal quote may have the ring of truth, but it doesn't adequately convey the importance of African-American blues and culture. That was my mission on my blues show. In order to entertain, educate and elevate, I provided blues information, history, and the best damn blues around from every region, style, and era.

THE BLUES ON WBFO

In America, we all grow up in the musical shadow of the red, the white, and the blues. One of the best things about my blues show was the sense of community that it developed almost immediately. People called me on the phone, e-mailed me, and came up to me at clubs and concerts to tell me how much they loved hearing the blues. And I loved playing them.

I was always prepared. Arriving at the station, I'd be carrying a bag of books, a three-ring binder filled with notes, and at least four bins of CDs. Each week I spotlighted a featured blues artist throughout the show. The show was too short to fit everything I wanted to say and play, though. Blues fans and Western New York Blues Society members were always

"Are you ready for the blues?!"

clueing me in to some new artist, and I'd include them in my show. Dennis Foster of the Blues Society went so far as to make a mix-CD of his blues favorites. It reminded me of my first year playing underground music at WYSL, when a fan spoke to me on campus and asked if we had *Aoxomoxoa*, the third Grateful Dead album. Sure enough, when I got to the station, that album was in our library and I played it.

Blues record labels loved to double dip with their artists. This means they released an album by one of their artists, and then later released a compilation album of various performers to make more money out of the same songs. It didn't cost them any more since they already owned and had paid for the masters. One day, while playing a track from one of these albums, I thought, why can't we put together a compilation album? I made a couple of calls to some friends in the industry and the blues ball started rolling.

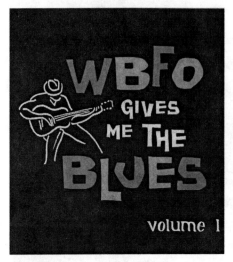

Within a year of the initial idea, WBFO embarked on a challenging yet successful project that would showcase local blues bands. We produced our own blues albums: *WBFO Gives Me the Blues*. The first album was produced through Alligator Records. The rest were all locally produced. There are seven volumes in all. I never dreamed it would go beyond one or two volumes. Station manager Dave Benders, music director Bert Gambini, and pledge producer Joan Wilson took the ball and ran with it. I doubt this would have happened at any other station.

Hundreds of songs were submitted by local blues musicians. We were beginning to live up to our slogan: "Buffalo's Home of the Blues." We used the CDs as pledge premiums. We even sweetened the pot by adding "WBFO Gives Me the Blues" T-shirts. We consistently went over our fundraising goals. I always found it difficult to wear the T-shirt comfortably, though. Whenever I put one on, my chest would swell to breaking! It wasn't enough to just play the blues, what really mattered to me was that we played a lot of local blues artists.

It was always exciting to introduce unknown blues artists. Kelley Hunt was one of my early favorites. I couldn't play enough of her. Come to find out, listeners couldn't get enough of her either. Part of her common appeal was an eight-minute original blues tune that chronicled her style as a creative pianist and singer with roots in the Kansas City boogie-woogie tradition. She credited her teacher, Mary Burke Norton, with a tribute titled *Queen of the 88s*. As a matter of fact, when Kelley played her first Buffalo concert, which was at Nietzsche's, she was amazed at how many people could sing the lyrics to her songs. When she asked the audience how they knew so much of her music, they called out my name, WBFO, and my blues shows. She played. We met. I fell in love. Before I knew it we had adopted each other.

The Western New York Blues Society, which numbered around 800 members at that time, sent a local band to a national competition each year. There was always a spot for local music on my show. In 2003, the Blues Society awarded me the *Blues Beat Magazine Muddy Waters Award* for my efforts in promoting and supporting the blues.

With the Queen of the 88s, Kelley Hunt.

GROWING AN AUDIENCE

Soon it wasn't just me asking, "Are you ready for the blues?" Listeners would greet me at concerts and events with my own catch phrase. Within a few years, the *Blues* was one of WBFO's most popular shows. At pledge time, it wasn't unusual to raise $10,000 during one four-hour shift.

A live broadcast at the Elmwood Avenue Festival of the Arts, 2005.

> "The blues became a ratings powerhouse, making WBFO a top five radio station in the Buffalo market on Saturday afternoons."
> (Mark Scott, WBFO)

My work was rewarded when an extra hour was added to my Saturday show. Within a few years, WBFO added a Sunday blues show and my hours doubled. When you added those hours to a 10 p.m.-to-midnight Saturday and Sunday show hosted by Debbie Sims, WBFO played fourteen hours of blues each weekend.

BETWEEN A ROCK AND A HARD PLACE

In the summer of 2008, I had a knee replaced. I planned to be off the air for two months. Part-timers would fill in for me. By September, I was back to work on Saturdays. When the recovery period stretched on, the station's concern for my health and more importantly their need for a Sunday blues host prompted the hiring of 97 Rock's Anita West in the spring of 2009. I worked Saturdays and she worked Sundays. Ironically, I had just made the decision to tell them I was ready to come back full time.

To complicate matters, rumor had it that the University at Buffalo was going to sell WBFO. Many off-air employees started looking for new jobs and weren't replaced. In late 2009, a hatchet-wielding consultant was brought in. Station employees were offered incentives to retire early. A full-time staff of fourteen was reduced to seven. Only three tenured positions were ensured university jobs. Rumor had turned into fact. The future of the blues show was up in the air.

When WBFO was sold to WNED in 2012, there was an all-out campaign to keep the blues alive, spear-headed by Anita. In all honesty, I believe that WNED CEO, Don Boswell, and his staff were not fully aware of the blues shows' popularity. To their credit, they took the time to evaluate the situation and ended up keeping the blues programming.

The blues show moved with the sale, and so did Anita and I. The bad news was that we lost our prime afternoon hours. The blues moved to Saturday and Sunday evenings from 7 p.m. to midnight. This was when we found out just how well the blues fit into the afternoon hours. The biggest complaint we heard was we were on too late. Listeners preferred going to a club to hear live local blues bands than staying home and listening to the radio. Surprise, surprise.

It was around this time that my health began to deteriorate. I was diagnosed with atrial fibrillation, as well as Parkinson's disease, a degenerative neurological condition. The combination caused my physical coordination and vocal performance to suffer. It made speaking clearly and coherently difficult. I hated the fact that I could not measure up to my self-imposed high standards. It finally got to the point where I had to make a decision. I was caught between a rock and a hard place.

In the fall of 2012, WBFO offered me a new contract and a pay raise. But I had made the decision to retire. On December 1, 2012, I said goodbye to my loyal blues and radio fans who had supported me for more than four decades. It wasn't easy.

When I was interviewed about my retirement, I was asked: "Why do you think your fans are so loyal?" I told the journalist that I had never been just an announcer. I talked to my audience as though they were friends sitting across from me in my living room. I've always felt that intimate connection with listeners. Radio and music have been the two greatest passions of my life.

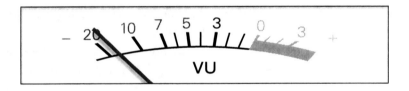

NINETEEN

For Radio Freaks Only: The Summary

If you think you know how a successful FM radio station is programmed, stop reading, break open your piggy bank, get in touch with me, and let's go out and buy a radio station. Maybe you can teach me something. Or if you're a radio freak like me, read on. Maybe I can teach you something—like why radio is so boring these days.

Let's climb into the "Way-back Machine." Destination: the Golden Age of Radio. The 1930s and 1940s were filled with artistic variety. In the 1950s, with the rise of television, those AM shows faded and were replaced by music programming. One disc jockey playing music was a lot less expensive than paying for all of the various talents needed for a half hour comedy, drama, or live music show. Teenaged listeners replaced family listening. Sponsors like Lux soap, Ipana toothpaste, and Doan's Little Pills were replaced by ads for Brylcreem, acne medications, and transistor radios. AM programming was king. In the late 1960s, music became the perfect vehicle for FM radio. Music grew up. In Buffalo, college-aged listeners switched from WKBW-AM to WPHD-FM.

Radio is both an art form and a business. The first commercial radio station was Pittsburgh's KDKA-AM in 1920. The first broadcast, the Harding/Cox election results, was voiced by Leo Rosenberg, radio's first announcer/engineer. The first paid radio commercial was aired in August 1922 on WEAF-AM. By the 1990s, it wasn't unusual for stations to play a ten commercial stop set. But business has been a part of radio practically from the beginning.

Radio listeners often say they prefer FM over AM radio. These days, the common opinion is that AM is for talk shows and FM is for music. It has to do with how the signal is transmitted and what is transmitted. It's kind of like the difference between a sunny and a rainy day. The FM signal is clean and bright and sounds better.

Enter FM radio pioneer Edwin Armstrong who originally developed FM radio in the 1930s. It was static free. Unfortunately, the frequencies he developed were suspended during World War II. After the war, RCA's David Sarnoff and Armstrong tenaciously fought over control of the FM radio band. The FCC granted Sarnoff the right to broadcast TV on Armstrong's original FM frequencies. On June 27, 1945, the new FM radio frequencies were reassigned. So by midcentury, Armstrong was forced to redevelop a new FM band farther up the dial. Can you believe it? He developed FM radio twice!

Stations that applied for an AM license automatically got an FM license as well. Usually FM ran the same shows as their AM sister station twenty-four hours a day. There was no extra cost involved. In 1966, the FCC called an audible. They ruled that broadcasters who owned both AM and FM stations must start broadcasting at least six hours of separate programming on FM. Eventually, that became twenty-four hours a day. The door was wide open for new programming.

College students and West Coast Top 40 DJ burnouts were the first to take advantage of the programming opportunity, playing what they wanted without any restrictions. Overnight, FM DJs developed a new style and the new freeform format. It was destined from the start to become a battle between the art of radio and the business of radio.

Whether it was West Coast jocks like KMPX-FM's Tom "Big Daddy" Donahue and KPPC-FM's B. Mitchell Reed or East Coast contemporaries, WNEW-FM's Scot Muni and Alison "Your Night Bird" Steele, you sensed that there was a human being behind your speakers, one with a heart as well as warts. Some would say that the Golden Age of Radio represented the height of the art of radio. But for me and my generation of DJs, that was really the underground years. The freedom to explore musical, political, and social themes only lasted about six years. In some markets, even less than that. I survived.

Let's face it, my type of jock faded quickly. Many early freeform jocks, to stay in the business, had to turn their backs on the art of radio and embrace the business of radio, touting formats, charts, and ratings. By the mid-1970s, management had regained control of programming and, if jocks wanted to keep their jobs, they had to conform. They were like the Rolling Stones' "Under Assistant West Coast Promotion Man" ("I'm a necessary talent behind every rock and roll band"). Eventually, even I had to succumb.

What was once an underground movement morphed into a Top 40 format of album-oriented music. Lee Abrams was the architect of the SuperStars format. Everything changed. Some would say for the better; some would say for the worse. To give the devil his due, the format succeeded. What this did was expand the listening audience and therefore guarantee a solid advertising base.

Here is a brief timeline of AOR (Album-Oriented Radio), as I lived it:

1969–1972: Total freeform music programming
1972–1974: Not freeform, but still underground/progressive
programming
1974–1975: Nine-month period, freeform with just a touch of control
1975–present: Corporate rock

Lee Abrams took Top 40 programming principles and transferred them to FM. DJs began to read and choose music first from 3x5 cards, and later from computer-generated lists. Many shows are tracked.

MOVING ON

Radio had become all business. In hindsight, it had almost always been business over music. For the jaded music enthusiast, music was just the noise that separated the commercials. Where do you find the balance between the business and the art?

Personally, I believe the crippling blow was delivered when the Telecommunications Act of 1996 allowed radio or TV groups to own more than one station in a market. The idea was to encourage more competition. When I was younger, WKBW-AM, WYSL-AM, WBEN-AM, and WEBR-AM fought tooth and nail to attract as many listeners as possible in order to turn their listeners into advertising dollars. In retrospect, it kept radio stations on their toes. Today, if a station loses listeners it doesn't make that much difference because most of the money goes into the same pot. At this time, in the Buffalo market, Entercom and Cumulus dominate. Now we have just a handful of local owners serving the needs of our entire community.

To this day, one of my radio heroes is Ramblin' Lou Schriver. He has owned WXRL-AM since 1970, one of the few independently owned and operated local stations in Western New York. Ramblin' Lou has been inducted into both the Buffalo Broadcasters Hall of Fame and the Country Music DJ Hall of Fame. Larry Green, who owns WLVL-AM, WECK-AM and FM is another example of local ownership. These stations exemplify local programming. WLVL's website even says: "We're dedicated to providing Niagara County with programming that keeps residents informed and entertained." It's a David and Goliath situation. That's the company I want to be in. In the early 1970s, I looked into buying my own radio station. Unfortunately, the cost, a reasonable $250,000 at the time, was about $249,000 more than I had. My dream of a Jim Santella progressive rock station, WSAN, died.

The gap between the art and the business of radio is even wider now. There used to be live DJs twenty-four hours a day. Though morning shows on most FM stations are still broadcast live, now more and more air time is tracked material, much of it syndicated. Technological advances in digital recording make it simple to program. With drag and drop capabilities, one jock can record a six-hour show in less than ninety minutes.

Jocks don't pick their own music, words, or thoughts anymore. It used to be that between the diet soda, savings bank, and automobile spots, a landscape of fun, music, and, yes, even some humanity could be heard. I used to love to hear the banter between the freewheeling Danny Neaverth and Sandy Beach. They even knew how to pronounce Scajaquada! Today, corporate consultants, social media, and electronic syndicated fact sheets make all jocks sound like they're reading from the same script.

On January 9, 1999, I completed exactly thirty years to the day in commercial radio with the final broadcast of *Radiation Theater*, my freeform, must-hear music show on 97 Rock that was patterned after my early days at WPHD-FM. I had total freedom to play anything (within reason). Ninety Seven Rock's program director, John Hager, trusted me not to embarrass him on the air, and in return I was given the keys to the music vault and permission to spotlight my own extensive library. John kept a low profile, but as the ultimate professional, he always seemed to do the right thing. I didn't get fired or walk off the air that time. It was just time for me to move on.

I was certainly charmed by other artistic projects that were presented to me. I was beginning to think more seriously of myself as a writer. The idea of writing my memoir actually began at this time. It only took seventeen years to write and seven decades to live!

I wanted to focus more of my energy on the blues. Developing the blues show on WBFO-FM for fifteen years was a perfect example of what could happen with artistic freedom. Left to my own devices, it was disciplined, yet unrestricted, and continued to succeed and grow in popularity year after year.

If I were driving the magic radio bus today, I would hire and trust knowledgeable disc jockeys who know both radio and music. One size does not fit all. I'd hire talented, conversant, curious individuals who want to explore and push the edge without driving the bus over the cliff. But, of course, talent costs money.

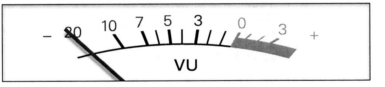

TWENTY

Demon in Disguise

Radio is the ideal medium for performers who need to hide their good looks behind a microphone. Take me, for instance. I truly have a face made for radio. I'm really a demon in disguise.

Don't let the glasses fool you
Stand beside me when you measure my size
Don't let false estimations rule you
'Cause even you will come to realize

I've been a wizard since my childhood
And I've earned some respect for my art
I rule the spirits that live in the wild
And every evening I talk to the stars…

I really think you should have guessed by now
That I am a Demon in Disguise
You're just a lit bit behind all the rest somehow
I mean you miss all the hints that show the truth to the wise

(David Bromberg, "Demon in Disguise," 1972)

I am and always have been a soft-spoken man. All my life people have said to me, "I love your voice. It's so smooth and easy to listen to." I was able to capitalize on that. Folks felt like I was the guy next door, that they could trust me. It gave me a boost. When one is in the studio for hours at a time, there is a sense of ease and freedom that comes with connecting with the audience. The emphasis is on the words, not how one looks.

"He [Jim Santella] had a warmth about him. An inclusiveness and friendliness. He's Italian and he likes to talk," said Pat Feldballe, who will replace Jim as host of the *Saturday Blues* show ...

Former WBFO *Spoken Arts* host, Mary van Vorst, agrees.

"He loves radio. He breathes radio." said van Vorst. "It's inconceivable to me that he would not be on the radio."

(Mark Scott, WBFO's website, November 30, 2012)

My fans have also always kept me on my toes. Let me give you an example.

One night at the Lafayette Tap Room while waiting for Coco Montoya to perform, I noticed a young female blues fan trying to catch my eye. I was flattered. She was more than attractive; she was downright alluring. She eventually made her move and sidled up to me.

"Are you Jim Santella?" she cooed.

"Yes."

"The guy with the blues show?"

"Yeah. Do you enjoy the show?"

"My mother says she used to date you! She says Hi!"

That knocked the wind out of my sails. Suddenly I felt like I was a hundred years older than her, rather than twenty-five. But it did remind me I'd been playing music for a long time. With forty-five years in broadcasting, the grandchildren of my original listeners could be listening to me play the blues!

Perhaps this is the time to reveal that being a DJ had its perks. Yes, we got free concert tickets. Yes, we got free albums. Yes, listeners bought us drinks. And yes, sometimes, women wanted to meet the man with, "the face made for radio." I met and dated my fair share of women over the years. I wasn't naive enough to believe it was my boy-band looks that got me dates. My friend Mary van Vorst always warned me to check their licenses for their real age. The standard joke for years among my relatives was "Who is Jim going to bring to the family get-together this Christmas?"

Once at a holiday party, shortly after we got engaged, Mary Lou came up to me and asked: "Are you 'The Stud of Buffalo?'"

"Not me!"

"Well, that's not what I heard in the ladies room!"

"Can't believe everything you hear."

To this day, I'm still not sure if it was true or if she was pulling my leg.

Of course, I still kid her about succumbing to the charms of John Astin; you know, Gomez on the 1960s sitcom *The Addams Family*. This is how it started: Astin appeared in a one-man show at Buffalo State's Rockwell Hall in 1998. I was on assignment to review him. Afterwards, we were invited to a small after-show party. Mary Lou, who looked particularly fetching in her short, black, bare-shouldered cocktail dress, was introduced to Astin—I thought she looked better than Morticia. You could see Astin's large eyes twinkle as he said, "Cara mia." Mary Lou melted. When he held her hand in his and slowly began planting kisses on her from her wrist to her shoulder, she was smitten. To this day, all I have to do is say, "Cara mia," and Mary Lou smiles at the memory.

Because I was there at the start and endured, I came to be known as the "Father of Progressive Rock" in Buffalo. That's quite an honor. Why did I survive so many years? The answer is simple. I stayed true to my own beliefs and shared them with the audience. I was consistent. By this time, it's probably pretty obvious that what got me into trouble, and fired from various stations, was a reluctance to follow what other people were doing. I always knew that if a crowd was marching down the street from left to right, that I should go from right to left. That doesn't necessarily mean I was correct. Yet, I never felt like a radical, I was just contrary. But if I had followed the rules, would you be reading this right now? Probably not.

AGE IS JUST A NUMBER

I've always lied about my age. I'm not proud of the deception but in my defense I've always felt that my chronological age and my maturity age were a decade apart. Actually, I really didn't lie about my age as much as *misled* people. When asked directly how old I was, my coy reply would be, "Age is just a number and mine is unlisted." Or I would answer their question with a question: "How old do you think I am?" They would inevitably reply with a number six to ten years short of my true age. I would reply, "Who told you?"

In all honesty, most of my friends knew I was playing fast and loose with my birth date. Why did I have such a concern for an inconsequential thing like that? Over the years I've gotten some insight into this failing of mine. My life seems to be divided into two eras: B.C.—before coming of age, and A.D.—after divorce.

I always thought I had to make something of myself. By the age of 28, I had failed as a musician, husband, and father. Suddenly, after almost three decades of mediocrity, I seemed to have a rebirth, a renaissance of creative success. I found inspiration in radio, music, writing, comedy, drama, and all of the wonderfully inventive arts I had dreamed about as a kid. I was no longer pretending to be a cowboy, musician, or character in one of the many books I read. I was living my dreams. Finding my place in the real world, I didn't always make the right choices or the most popular ones, but I did find myself. Eventually, I didn't have to hide behind the deception of age. It didn't happen in a month, a year, or a decade. There were periods of backsliding and doubt, but I became content with all of my experiences. Nowadays, if you ask me my age, my reply is thirty-nine. It worked for Jack Benny. Just kidding!

Age does have its benefits. The older one gets, the more awards people want to bestow on you. I hope I deserve them. In 2005, I was inducted into the Buffalo Broadcasters Hall of Fame. I was the first FM DJ to be so honored. That award means the world to me.

Flanked by good friends Al Wallack and Jim Pastrick, following the induction into the Buffalo Broadcasters Hall of Fame in 2005.

The following year, I was voted The Best Radio Voice by *Buffalo Spree* magazine readers. Finally, in 2013, I was inducted into the Buffalo Music Hall of Fame. I can only say thanks for it all. I am both proud of and humbled by these honors.

When I decided to retire, several articles appeared about my retirement in local newspapers. Buck Quigley of *ArtVoice* described my decision in an article on November 21, 2012:

> In person, Santella is as thoughtful and gentle as he comes off on the radio. A jazz drummer, he can talk very intelligently about music, referencing sometimes obscure examples of songs, or giving his theory on why the Yardbirds were the greatest rock and roll band. But he's also well versed in theater, and is happy to veer onto a tangent to describe the absurdist play *Six Characters in Search of an Author*, by Luigi Pirandello. His knowledge of cinema is equally extensive. We discovered we'd both studied film history at UB under Professor Brian Henderson in the Media Study Department during the 1980s.
>
> With such a fire burning in the mind, it may come as a surprise to learn that in two short weeks, Jim Santella will be retiring from his weekend blues show at WBFO, *The Home of the Blues*. For several years, he has been putting together mixes of blues artists ranging from the seminal to the contemporary. He has a specific fondness for the stripped-down acoustic players, whose work boils down the 12-bar blues to its bare essence, until the music's very simplicity creates its power.
>
> He feels, however, that he hasn't been at his best on the air in recent months.
>
> "And if I can't be at the top of my game, I've decided it would be best not to carry on with the show," he says.
>
> As we pour through scrapbooks meticulously compiled by his wife, Mary Lou, he elaborates at length over certain news clippings. Then, he delicately describes his current struggle with Parkinson's disease. He has some difficulty getting around. I ask him if that information is something he would like included in this interview.

> "It's not something I feel comfortable telling my listeners. So in a way, I'd like to use you, to get the news out there," he explains.
>
> … Tune in at 7 p.m. for the final show by this legendary local DJ, complete with stories toasting the man of the hour from over a dozen old radio friends who will be chiming in from San Francisco, Los Angeles, Mississippi, and elsewhere. It promises to be a moving broadcast, not to be missed by fans of real American music and the genuine disc jockey who has taken such pleasure sharing it with us on the airwaves over the years."

Radio and music are as addictive as any drug. Put them together, and you have a vehicle that creates a shared experience, a great society, a counterculture of acceptance and tolerance—a vocabulary of humanity, if you will. Now, who wouldn't want to play a part in that?

It is said that as we get older, mortality and fear replace youthful dreams of invincibility. Maybe. Of course, ego and a nagging fear that we've wasted our precious lives without leaving a worthwhile legacy also rears its ugly head.

Radio and music have been my life. I realized long ago that I won't win a Nobel Peace Prize or develop a cure for AIDS, cancer, or the common cold. My only claim to fame is that I had the great fortune to play music that meant a lot to "*My Generation.*"

I'd like to think that over the years, I've gotten more savvy and experienced. But if John McGhan, God rest his soul, were to ask me to do mornings at a freeform radio station again and take an $8,000 pay cut, I'd do it all over again in a heartbeat.

Remember—without a little madness you can't be free.

EPILOGUE

Mary Lou says that I am a glass-half-full kind of guy. I'd like to think so. When I was a kid I remember my parents saying: "Be glad you've got your health." Too frequently we don't appreciate what we have until we lose it. Given all the activities I was involved in, I was always blessed with good health. But now, I am reconsidering my beloved Uncle George's words, "Growing old is not for the faint of heart."

Back in 2008, while recovering from knee surgery, my progress was going slower than expected. By early 2009, after more than one health care provider asked if I had Parkinson's, I finally got checked out. It was a big surprise to me, but they were right. Initially, I denied it. Oh, it's just my bad knees! I felt I had no other overt symptoms, except for the fact that I didn't swing my arms when I walked.

I guess I just learned to deal the hand I was dealt. Luck wasn't with me this time, but with perseverance and a positive attitude I decided I could deal with it. And I have. Parkinson's is a neurological disease which impairs movement. My limbs are stiff and I have difficulty walking and with balance. But, for me, the biggest drawback is that I no longer talk with my hands. I'm Italian, for heaven's sake. Now that's a challenge! I occasionally sit down at the drums to fiddle around, but it requires so much coordination of both hands and feet, that my skills are mostly a memory now.

Before we got married, the minister who performed our ceremony asked Mary Lou why she loved me. Her answer was: "He makes me laugh!" Laughter is the tonic to any illness, tragedy, or hardship; or simply a daily pick-me-up. Her answer must have been noteworthy, because when she reconnected with the minister years later, he remembered us by her response to his question.

That's my mission in life. To make Mary Lou laugh every day. She is a great help, since I can no longer drive and need help with certain daily activities. Oddly enough, she's been dealing with a chronic illness most of her life. She was diagnosed with Type 1 (insulin-dependent) diabetes in college. All of her exercise and carb counting has paid off, as she has no complications. We support each other. My dad had Type 1 diabetes long before the advances of today. He actually had to hide his illness for fear of losing his job as a teamster. He died of complications at age 57. Luckily, treatment options are much better now.

Mary Lou recently wrote this about me:

> Jim's outlook on life is always upbeat and I never hear him complain about his illness. He possesses an inner strength. He always tries to get me to see the positive. I want to be a "glass-half-full" kind of girl, but often cannot manage it without his help. Jim is kind, loving, and caring. He has taught me, in difficult situations to, as he puts it, "be the better person." And despite all of his success, he has always been a humble person and stayed true to his principles.

Together we'll see life through.

A portion of the proceeds from this book will be donated to the National Parkinson's Foundation and its Western New York affiliate.

INDEX

K

CPSIA information can be obtained
at www.ICGtesting.com
Printed in the USA
FFOW01n2308140517
35516FF

9 781942 483168